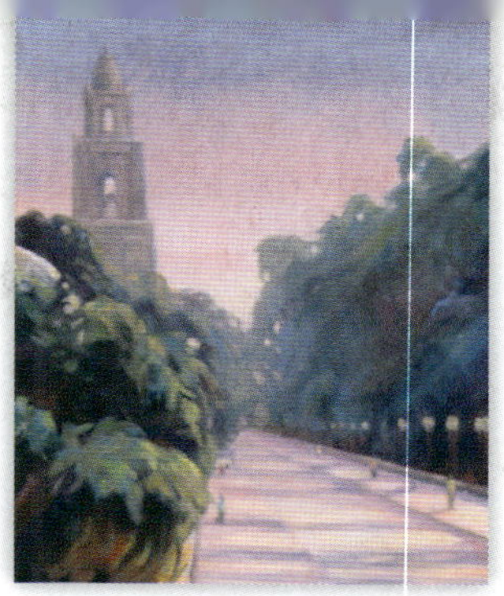

Acrylic 1

Acrylic is a very distinctive painting medium. In addition to having a unique look and feel of its own, it can also mimic other media, such as watercolor, oil, and even pastel. It's as convenient and quick-drying as watercolor and as permanent as oil and pastel. And it's extremely adaptable; it can be thinned to near transparency, or applied in thick strokes straight from the tube without any fear of it chipping or cracking over time. In this book, I will show you how the qualities of acrylic can be used to your benefit by keeping the paints moist, applying your colors in layers, and learning when to tone down the colors with neutrals. I'm confident that as I share with you what I know about acrylic paints, brushes, and techniques, you will agree that acrylic is truly one of the most enjoyable and versatile media on the market today. —*Ken Goldman*

CONTENTS

Walter Foster®

Supplies for Starters

ONE OF THE MOST WONDERFUL things about acrylic is its simplicity. You don't need a lot of fancy tools and bottles of additives—just paints and water will suffice. Still, I do have a few extras I like to use and a couple of tricks to share that will make your first acrylic painting experience a pleasant one. The basics listed here are all you need to get started, but if you're interested in learning more, see *Watercolor & Acrylic Painting Materials* by William F. Powell in the Artist's Library series.

▸ SUPPORTS Painting surfaces are often called *supports*. For acrylic, my favorite supports are toned, acid-free matte board, watercolor paper, and primed canvas (canvas that has a thin polymer coating), which are all readily available at art supply stores.

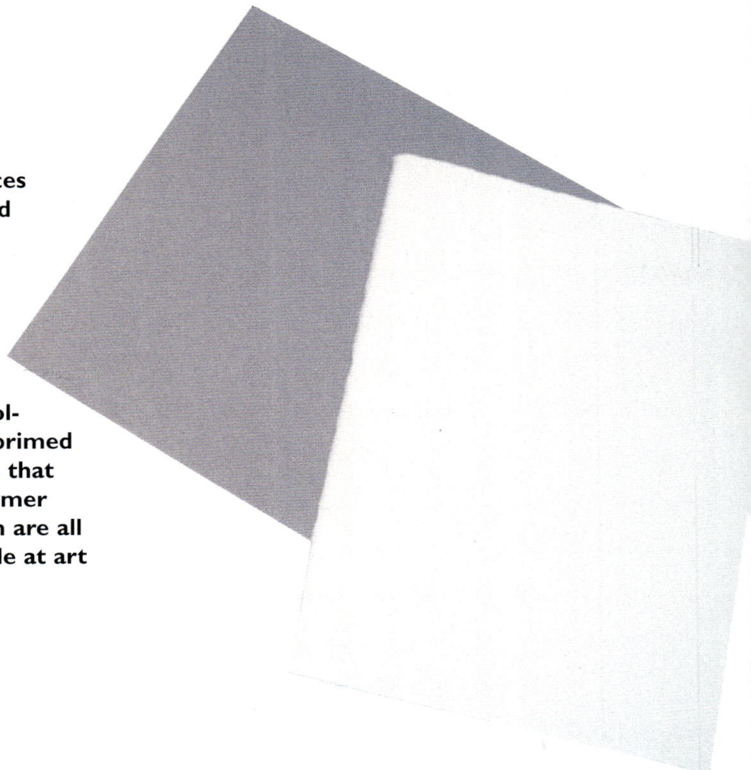

Acrylic Paints

Acrylic colors are available in tubes, jars, and cans, but I prefer tubes. I like being able to squeeze out as much or as little paint as I like, and tubes will seem more familiar to those of you who have worked in oil. You can get almost all the colors that are available in other painting mediums, with just a few exceptions. Still, you should be able to purchase or mix any color you will want or need.

▸ BRUSH HOLDERS I use water containers for storing my brushes, either in or out of water. While you're working, it's important to keep your brushes wet—and never let acrylic paint dry in the brushes, because it will ruin them. When you are finished painting for the day, be sure to wash your brushes in tepid (never hot!) water and lie them flat or hang them bristle-down to dry.

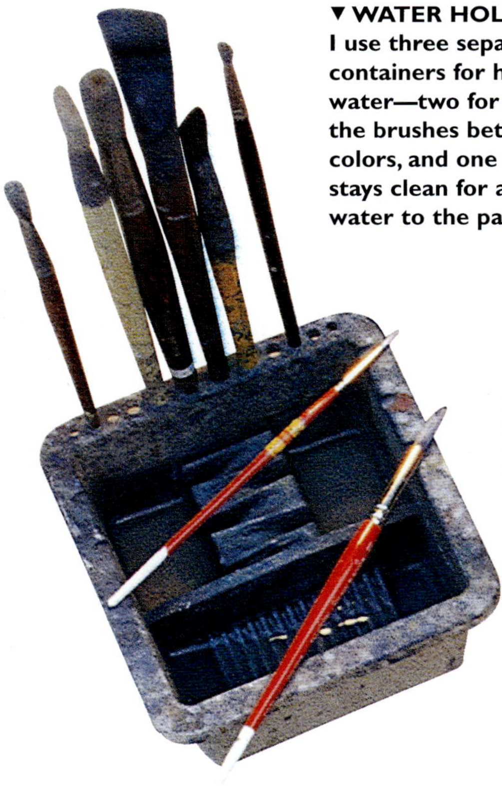

▾ WATER HOLDERS I use three separate containers for holding water—two for rinsing the brushes between colors, and one that stays clean for adding water to the paints.

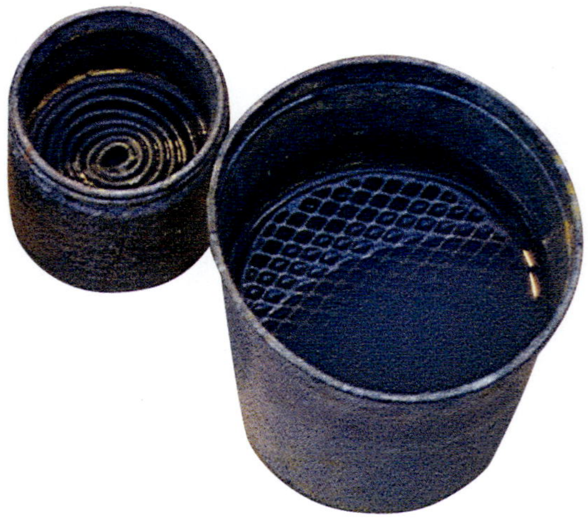

▸ ACRYLIC GESSO Gesso is the conventional material used for sealing and protecting fabric and wood supports (called *priming*). Although acrylic can be painted on unprimed canvas, gessoing provides a smooth surface and the right degree of absorption (see page 5).

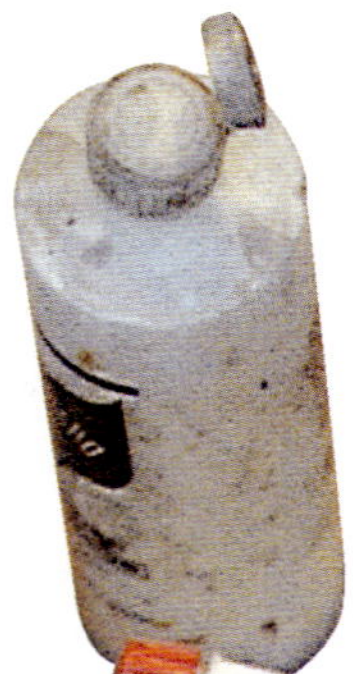

▾ SPRAY BOTTLE As I paint, I occasionally spray the paints with water so the air doesn't dry them out too quickly.

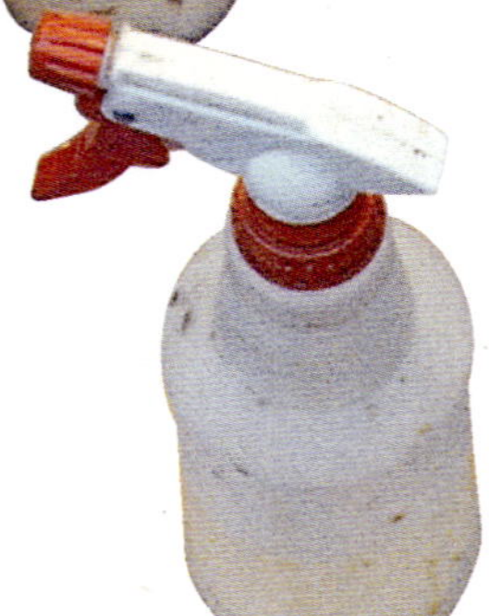

▸ MY STAY-WET PALETTE With this ever-moist palette, I can keep a lot of different colors ready to use. I don't mix my paints on this palette, though; I use a separate sheet of glass for that. I like using glass because the dried paint can easily be removed from it with a razor blade.

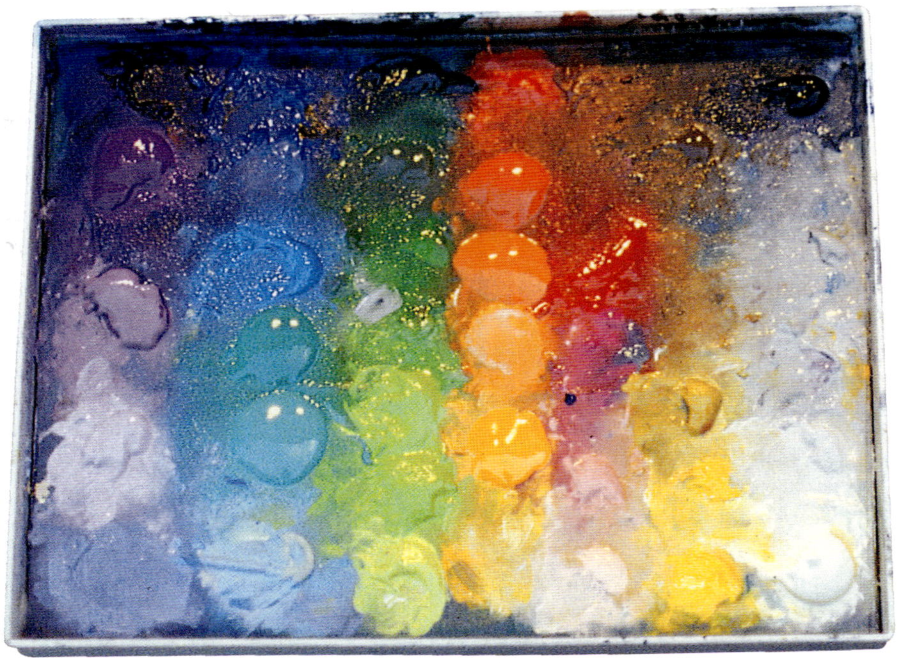

Keeping the Paints Moist

Acrylic paints dry quickly, so I have devised a "stay-wet palette" to keep them from drying out while I paint. I take a standard plastic palette container with an airtight lid and cut a piece of Plexiglas™ to fit inside. Then I put water in the palette container and place four thin sponges at each corner. Next I wet a piece of absorbent, white cotton fabric and put it on the Plexiglas, squeeze out my paints onto the fabric, and place the Plexiglas in the palette on top of the sponges. The sponges stay damp indefinitely and maintain a moist environment inside the container.

◄ CANVAS Whether linen or cotton, stretched canvas is the support that most acrylic painters use. You can buy a sturdy, deep 1-1/2" box canvas for your largest works or regular 3/4"-deep canvases for all other sizes. Store-bought canvases come already stretched and primed in all different sizes and formats, making them very convenient.

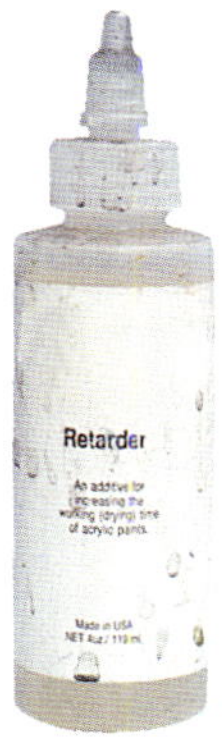

▼ RETARDER Acrylic retarder is an additive that slows the drying time of the paints. I never use more than a 15% solution, though, because too much retarder can create uneven drying problems.

Acrylic Brushes

If you don't mind spending more money, you can buy natural-hair brushes, but I use synthetic nylon brushes because they are economical and easy to keep clean. Also, they can be left sitting in water without swelling, the way bristle brushes for oils do. I use flat-style brushes for painting and blending large areas and pointed rounds for everything else. I suggest that you buy at least five or six different brushes, as shown here.

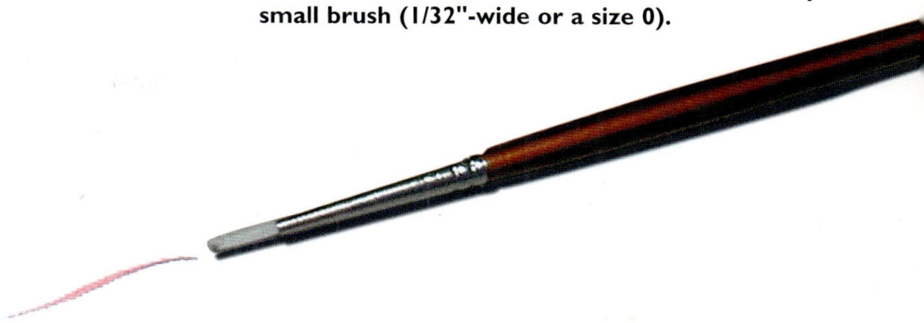

▼ SMALL POINTED ROUNDS If you do any small detail work, you will need at least one very small brush (1/32"-wide or a size 0).

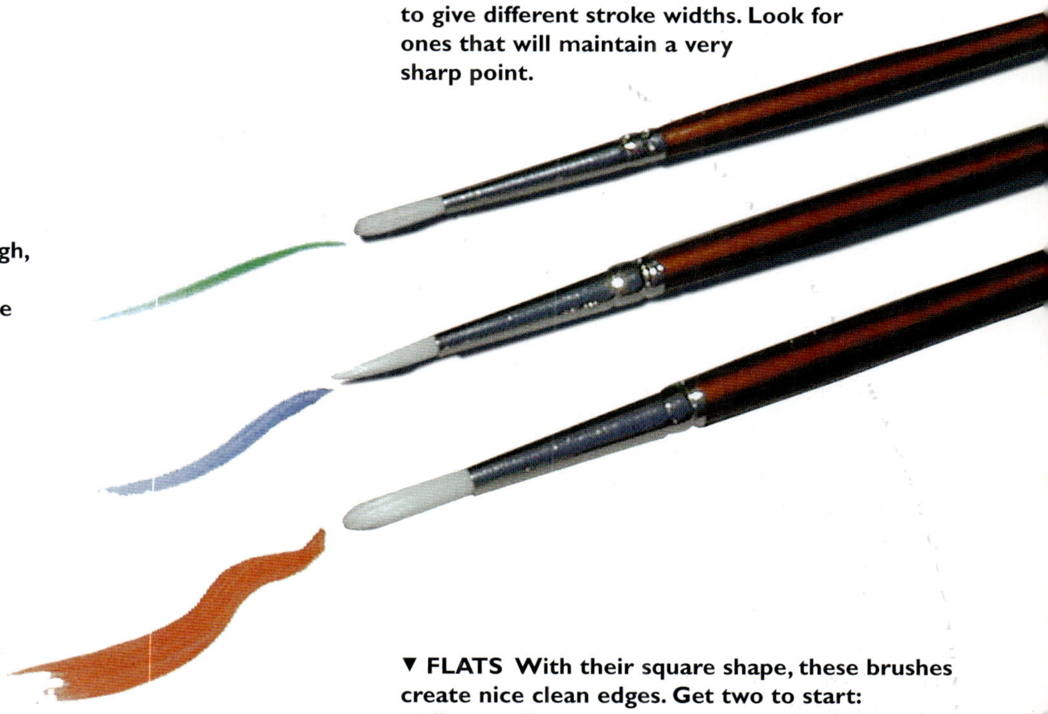

▼ POINTED ROUNDS You'll want a range of sizes—approximately 1/8", 1/4", and 3/8"—to give different stroke widths. Look for ones that will maintain a very sharp point.

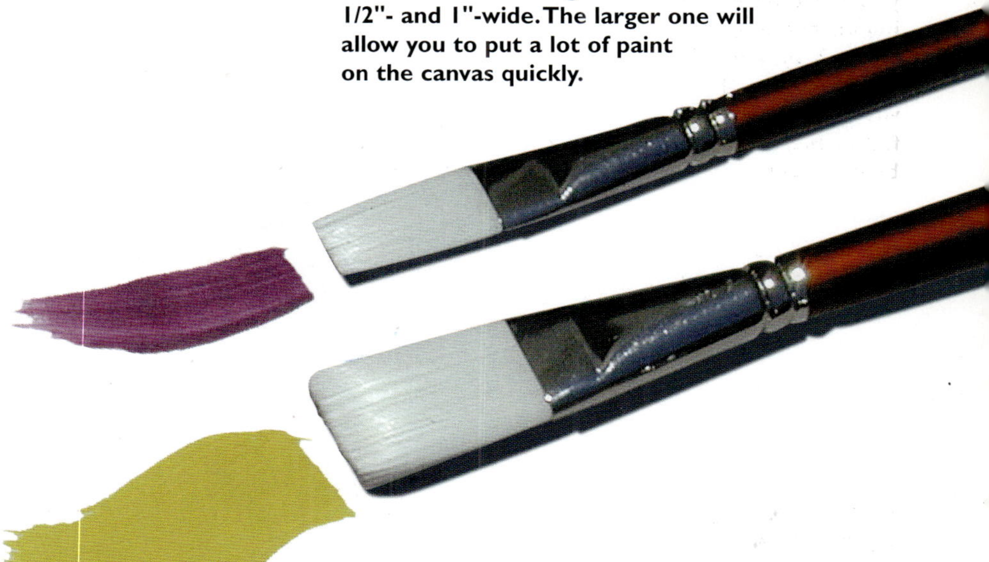

▼ FLATS With their square shape, these brushes create nice clean edges. Get two to start: 1/2"- and 1"-wide. The larger one will allow you to put a lot of paint on the canvas quickly.

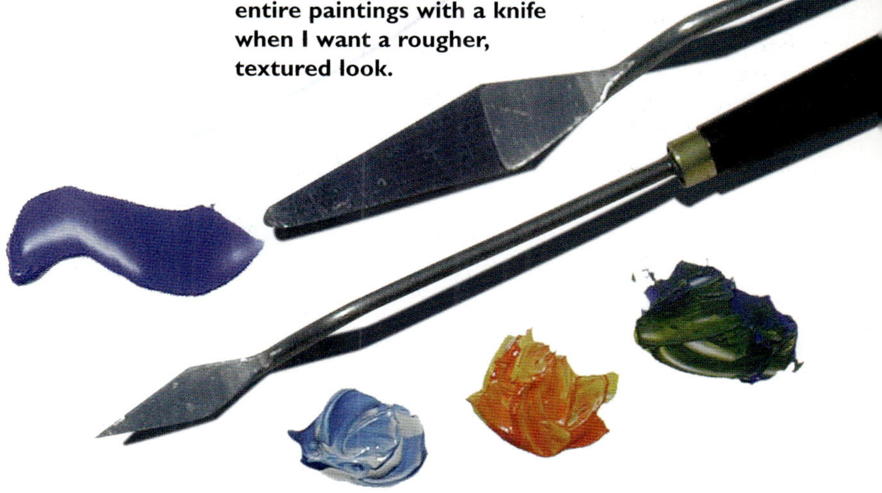

▼ PAINTING AND PALETTE KNIVES Palette knives are usually used for mixing paints on a palette, while painting knives are for applying paint to the support. Sometimes I use a knife only in areas where I want a lot of thick texture, but I also do entire paintings with a knife when I want a rougher, textured look.

My Basic Colors

There are so many bright, beautiful colors available that it may be hard to decide which ones to buy. I recommend starting with these basics: one yellow, a warm and a cool red, a warm and a cool blue, three earth tones, a white, and, if you like, a black.

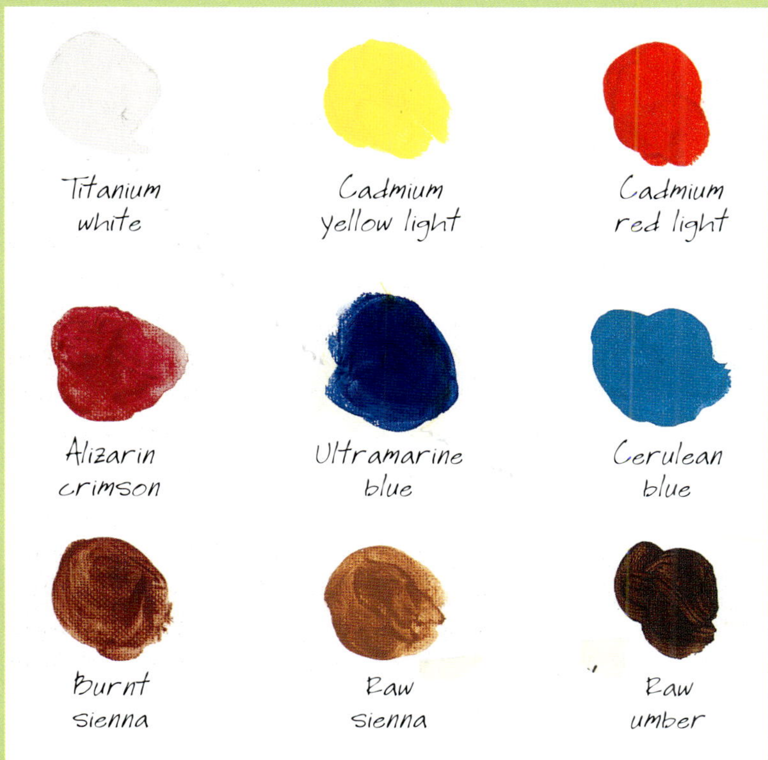

Taking the First Steps

STARTING A NEW PAINTING gives me a wonderful feeling. It's a combination of excitement, anticipation, and the joy of participating in a creative process. You may choose to start by warming up with sketches, or you may prefer to begin painting directly from life or from a photo—or even from a painting in a book, like this one. The important thing is to just jump in and get those creative juices flowing!

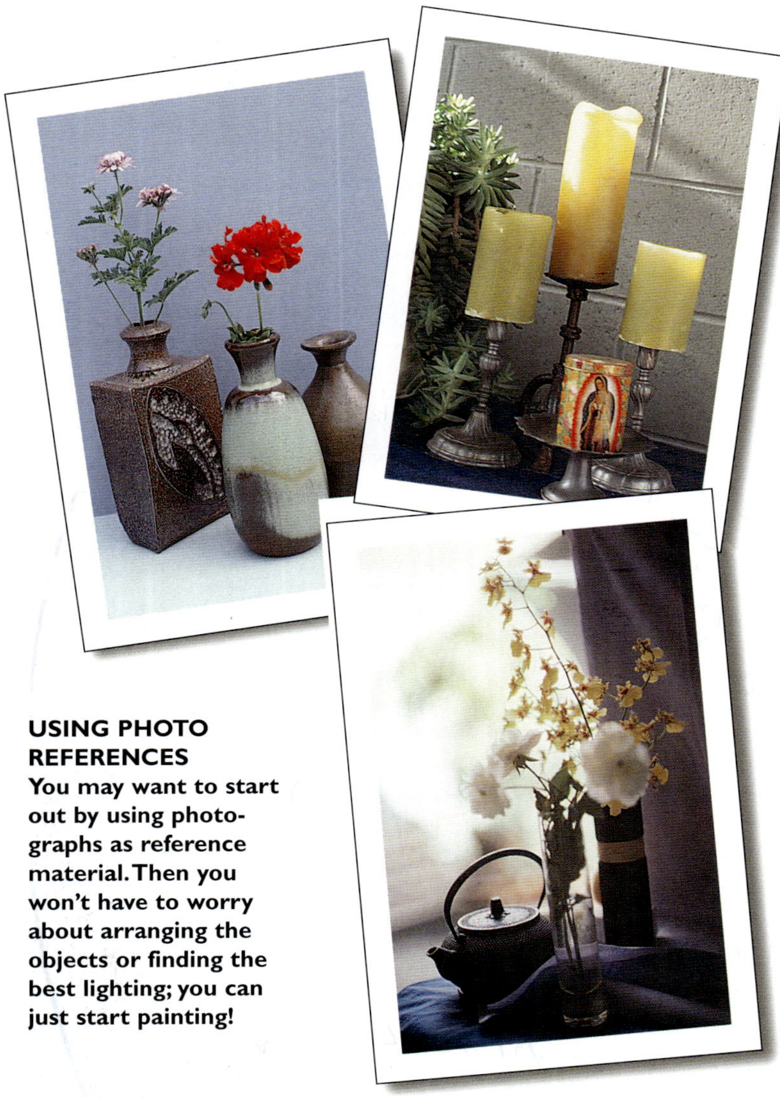

USING PHOTO REFERENCES **You may want to start out by using photographs as reference material. Then you won't have to worry about arranging the objects or finding the best lighting; you can just start painting!**

Using Acrylic Mediums

You can use acrylic in its pure form because it spreads fairly well, but if you're painting large areas, adding a painting medium will allow the acrylic to flow even more freely. Choose the type of medium that best suits your needs, and try a ratio of one part medium to one part paint. These are the different types of mediums: GLOSS medium extends paint and leaves a shiny surface. A small amount simply makes it easier to spread the paint around, whereas a large amount makes the color very transparent, which is great for glazing. MATTE medium works the same way gloss medium does but matte has a chalky talc added that reduces glare, so the surface won't be shiny. GEL medium acts the way matte and gloss mediums do, but gel also makes paint thicker, adding a textural effect. RETARDER slows drying time to make blending easier, but be careful not to add too much or your paints may dry unevenly.

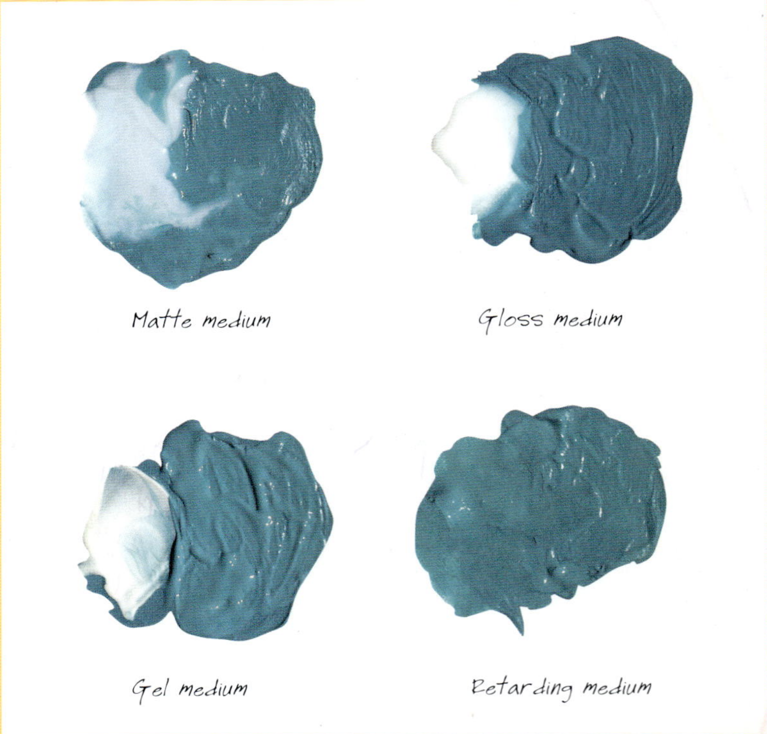

Deciding What to Paint

So how *do* you decide what to paint? I take a sketchbook almost everywhere I go so I can record ideas for future paintings, and I often take photographs and keep them in a file for source material. If you really look around, you can find interesting subjects that are close at hand, such as around your house or in your own backyard. Or you could collect ideas from books, magazines, newspapers—even calendars. And I bet if you went into the kitchen right now and started pulling things out of the cupboards, you'd have a terrific still life setup in no time. The important thing is to find something that interests you or has a special meaning to you—and if you're just learning to paint, keep things simple. Then the only problem will be narrowing your selection!

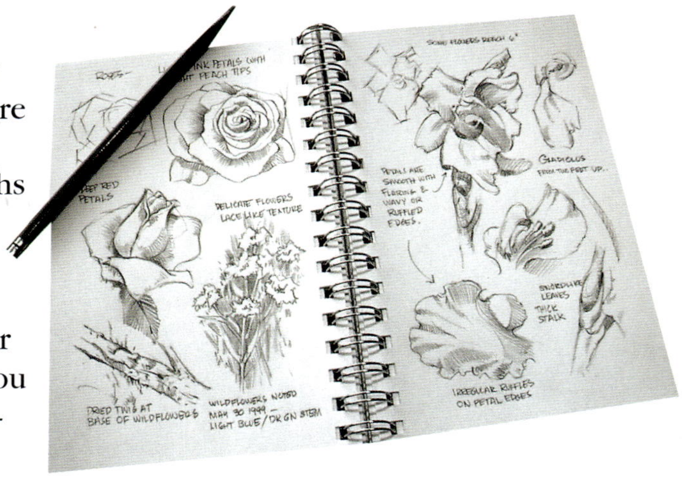

STUDYING YOUR SUBJECT **It's a good idea to study a variety of subjects and practice drawing them before starting a painting. I use a sketchbook, such as the one shown above, and go out in the field to draw from life to familiarize myself with as many different subjects as I can. I also make detailed notes about shape, color, and texture, which I find very helpful to refer to when I'm painting the subject back in my studio.**

Starting Out

Once you've chosen what to paint, do some quick pencil sketches before going to color. This is where you will determine the placement of your subject on the canvas and work out the correct shapes, proportions, and perspective. Then you're ready to draw directly onto the painting surface. Keep the shapes simple and blocky—there's no need to do a fully rendered drawing with shading and a lot of detail; you'll just paint over it anyway.

Once you're happy with your drawing, find a place with good lighting, gather all your painting materials, and make sure the telephone answering machine is on. Lay out the paints you want to use on your palette, and then follow the steps on page 5 to start painting!

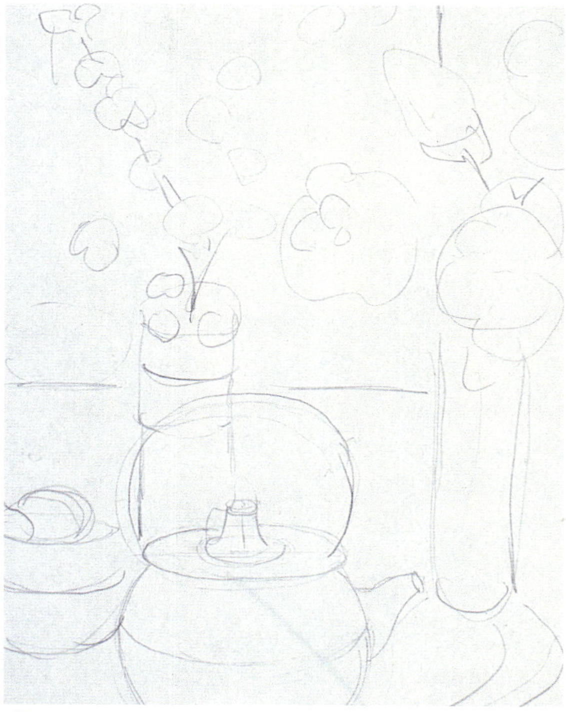

1 SKETCHING OUT I often sketch directly on my canvas using pencil or charcoal. Here I lightly sketched only the general outlines of the objects: the flowers and vases are simple circles and cylinders; the teapot is circles and ellipses with a spout. This sketch establishes the proportions and shapes and provides a guideline for applying color.

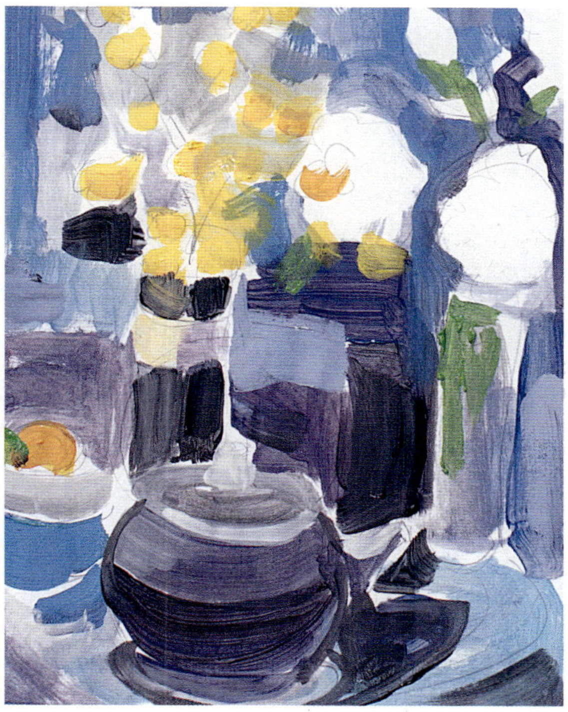

2 BLOCKING IN COLOR I begin painting by applying the most extreme colors first—both the darkest and the lightest areas. (These are easier to see if you squint your eyes.) I use a fairly large brush and work very loosely. The idea is just to get a base of all the right colors in the right places. Then I start making my shapes more accurate while still keeping my brushstrokes loose.

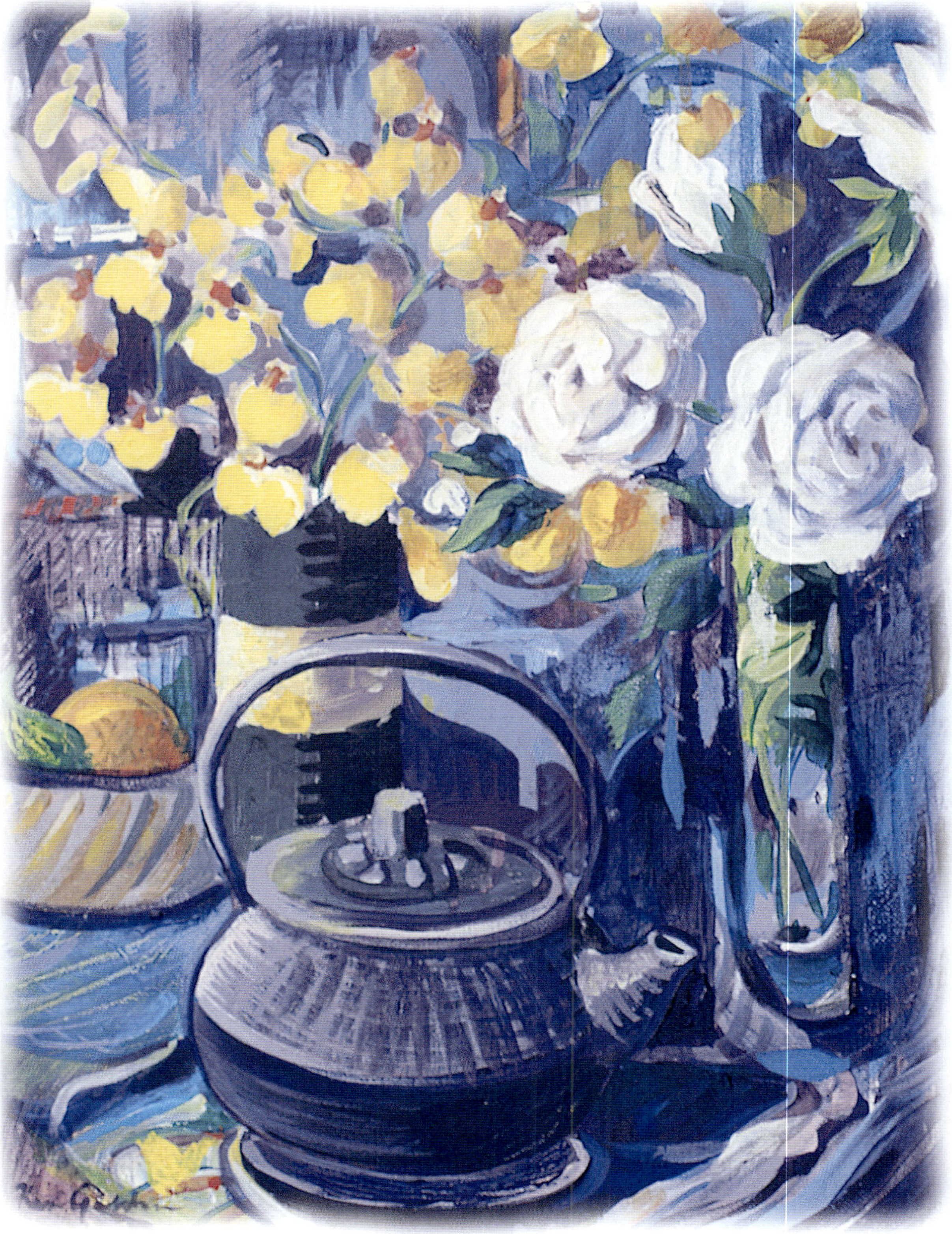

3 BEING IMAGINATIVE Feel free to *interpret* your reference rather than just copy it. Here I made the background much more active than it is in the actual photograph on page 4. I liked the backlighting of the photo, but decided to take a closeup view of the teapot instead.

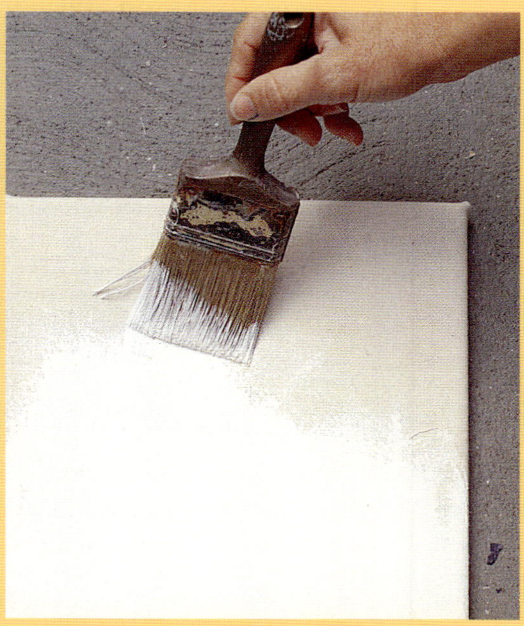

Priming Your Support

Preprimed supports are readily available at any art store, but you may prefer to prime the canvas or board yourself. To do this, you will need a hardwood board or stretched canvas, a jar of acrylic gesso, and a 2"-wide brush (a house painting brush works well).

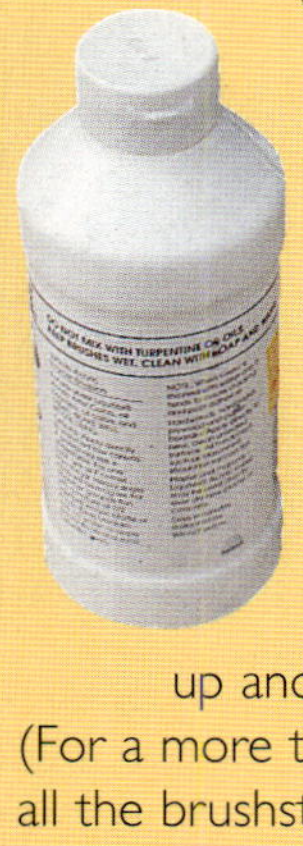

Pour some gesso directly on the support and spread evenly with the paintbrush, stroking alternately back and forth and up and down until the surface is smooth (For a more textured surface, don't smooth out all the brushstrokes completely.)

Artist's Tip

If you start with a charcoal sketch, be sure to paint over it with a layer of thinned acrylic to keep the charcoal from polluting successive colors.

Underpainting in One Color

I OFTEN START WITH A ONE-COLOR (monochromatic) base, so I can temporarily forget about what colors to choose and instead focus on the fundamentals: drawing, composition, and values. This base is called an *underpainting*, and it lays the drawing and value foundation for the actual colors I plan to use. You may not fully realize the power of values—the light, dark, and in-between shades of a color or of black—but they are what give shapes and colors dimension and life. And painting in one color is a fun and easy way to explore and learn about values.

Focusing on the Values

For a monochromatic underpainting, I choose a color, such as blue, and then develop a range of values: I add white where I want light areas and black where I want it darker and richer. The advantage of using only one color is that I can concentrate on establishing the correct values. The disadvantage is that a blue painting with white and blackish areas looks a bit raw. I prefer to start with a one-color underpainting and then add accents with contrasting colors at the end. Here I'll go through it step by step, so you can see how the values evolve.

Making Acrylic Colors Lighter or Darker

To darken a color as dark as ultramarine blue, only black or a very dark burnt umber or sepia can make it darker. To lighten it, however, you have two choices. The most obvious method is to add white, but since acrylics are water-based, they can also be lightened by adding water. However, do keep in mind that while adding water will lighten the values of your colors, adding too much water can weaken the strength of the polymer binder. Thin your paint color with a lot of water only at the beginning of a painting, and use painting mediums (see page 4) to thin color for the final layers.

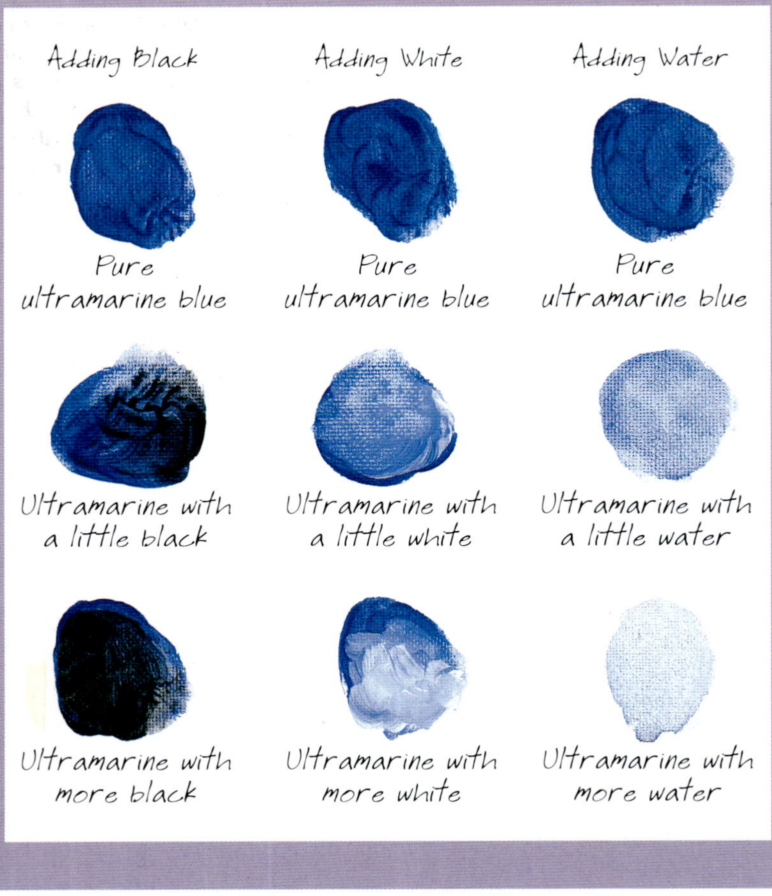

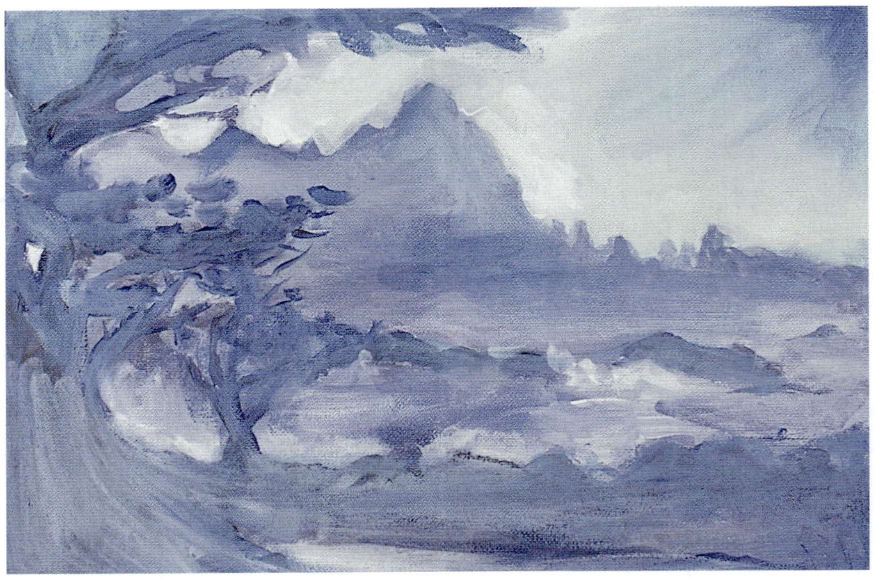

BLOCKING IN SHAPES As for any painting, I started with a sketch of the basic shapes. Here, on primed canvas paper, I drew with a brush and applied the paint in a very loose, free style—a "painterly" way of drawing.

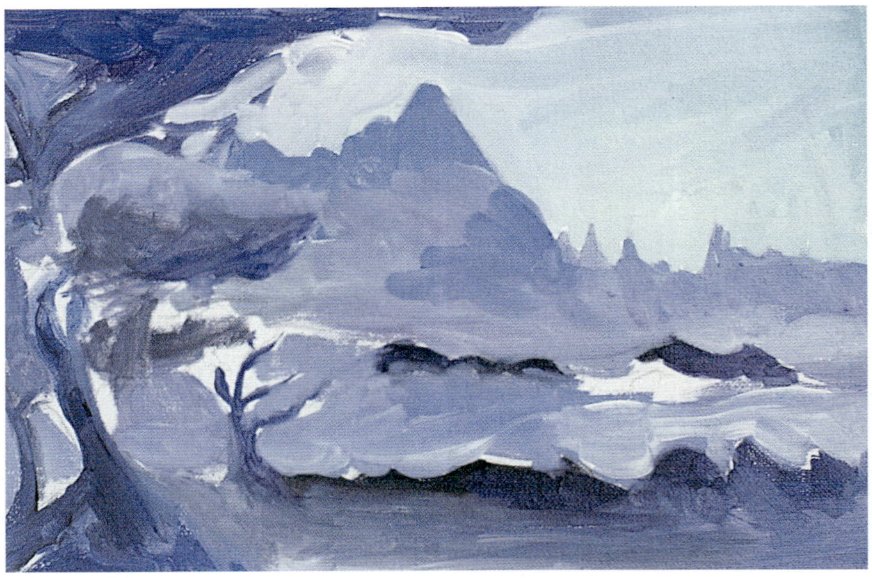

LAYING IN VALUES Now I began placing my dark values as accurately as possible. Acrylics are very opaque and dry quickly, so this stage is a matter of refining the shapes and edges until I think they are right; when needed, I correct a dark edge with a light edge, and vice versa.

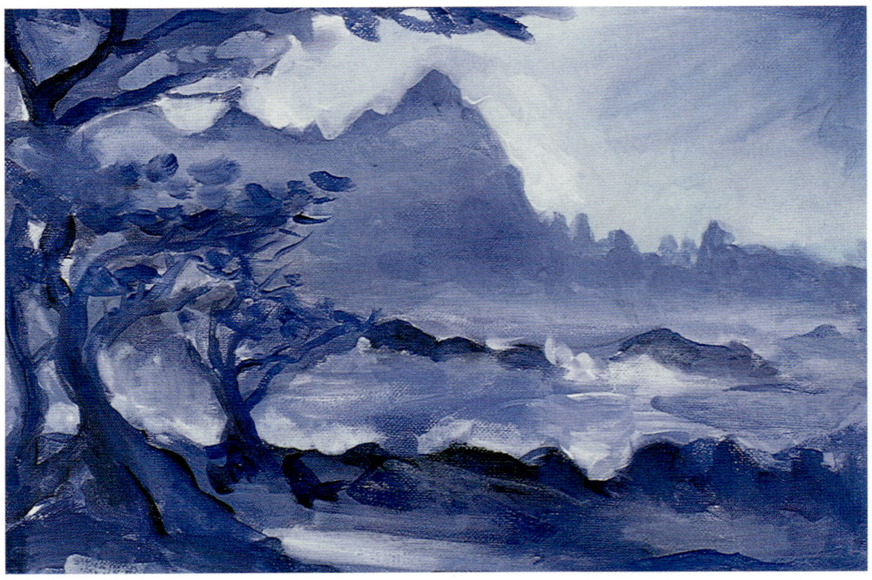

FINALIZING THE UNDERPAINTING By this stage, I could see that the values were working, but the intense blues and white sky looked too raw and pasty to me. A lot of artists do make complete paintings in one color, but I wouldn't choose to do a monochromatic painting in such an intense blue. For me, the painting at this point is a good underpainting, but not a finished piece of art. It needs more color and paint texture.

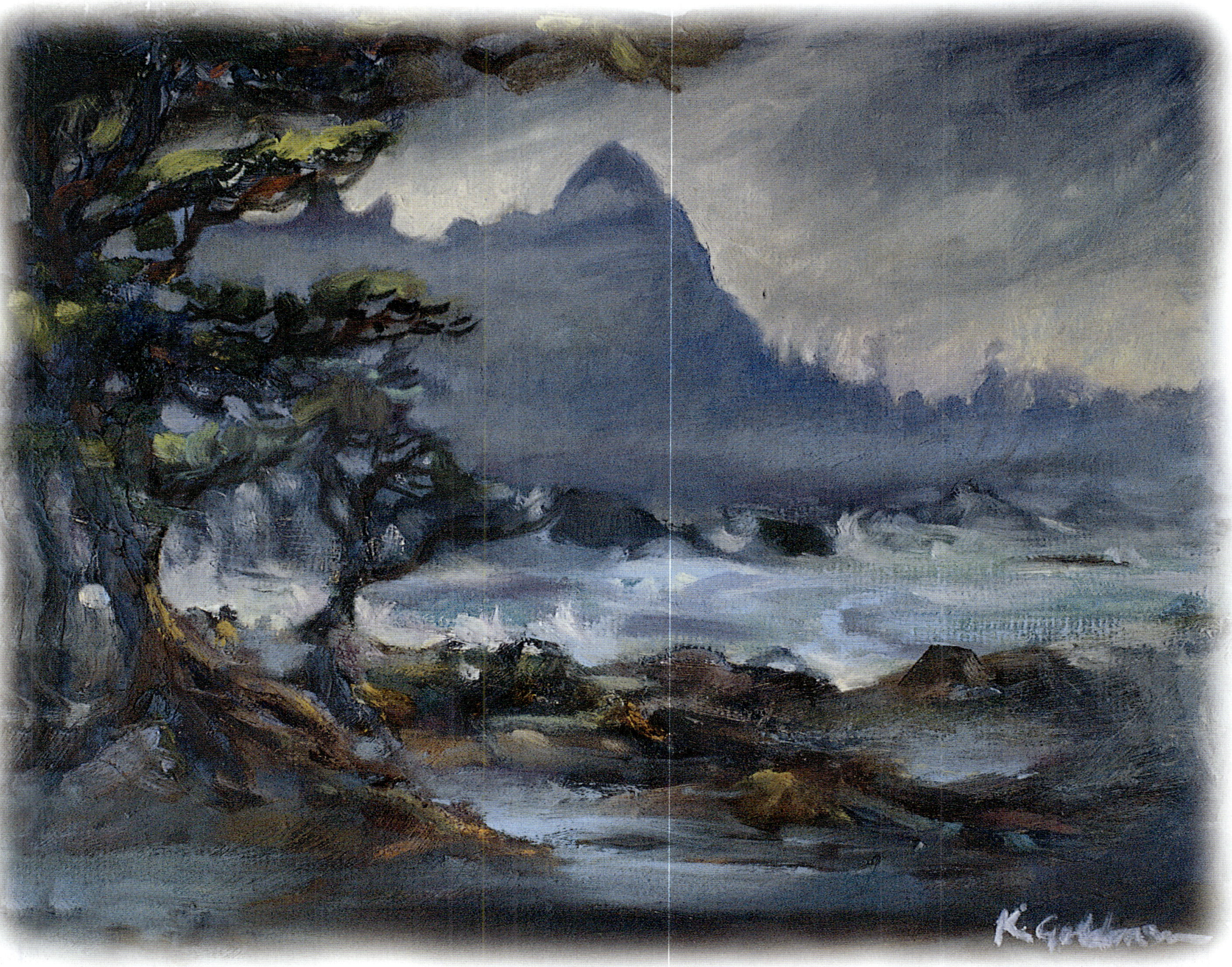

FINISHING WITH COLOR The additional touches of raw umber, yellow ochre, and cadmium yellow light give this painting a more refined look.

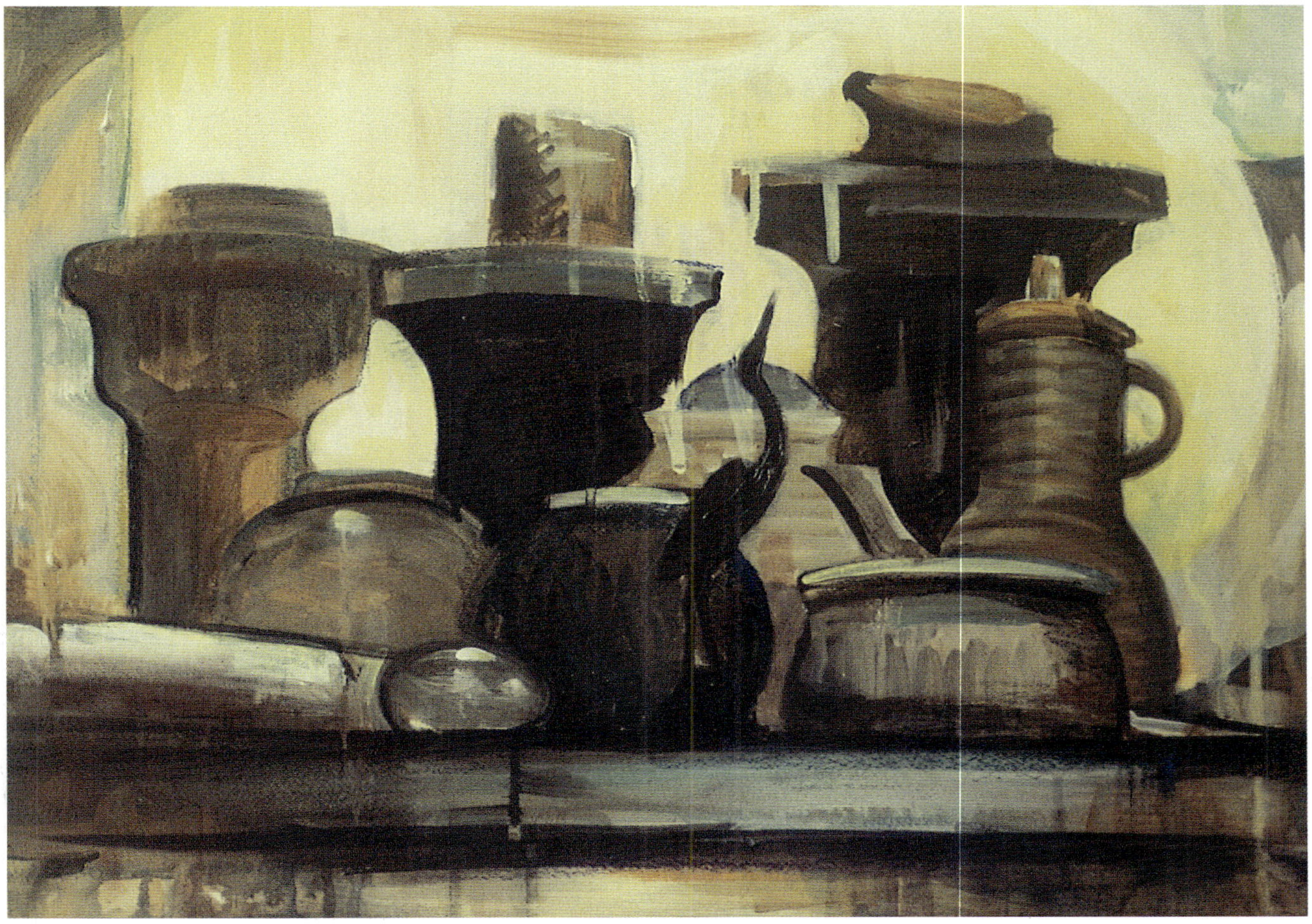

◄ **WORKING WITH A LIMITED PALETTE** Here's another example of a painting done in basically one color, but this time in shades of brown instead of blue. I like its bold, graphic quality and the fact that it derives its strength from value and composition, rather than from a multitude of colors.

Artist's Tip

If your subject has mostly earth tones, underpaint with a neutral color, such as raw umber or a mixed gray.

Developing Patterns and Textures

ACRYLIC IS A VERSATILE MEDIUM, which makes creating different textures a breeze. You can apply it in thick strokes or nearly transparent washes, and it can look smooth and glossy or rough and unpolished. Animals are great subjects for exploring textures in acrylic. What I enjoy most about painting them is the wide variety of shapes, textures, and colors I can create without being overly concerned with capturing an exact likeness. I've never had an animal complain that I made its nose too big or its tail too small!

Building Up the Textures

There is a tendency in rendering fur, scales, feathers, or what have you, to immediately start painting all the details. Resist the temptation. The way I make animals—or any subject with textures—look realistic is to first make an accurate drawing and then build up the forms slowly in a general way, with lights, shadows, and highlights. Then, with this firm foundation in place, I add hairs, scales, feathers, patterns, or whatever texture is called for. Think of the texture as a finishing touch you add at the end, rather than the whole reason for the journey. Below are a few techniques for painting a variety of textures you can use for any subject.

Creating Texture with Pumice

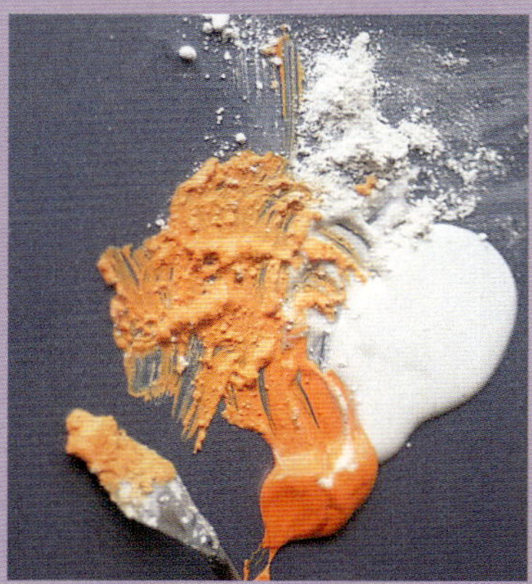

I have found that pumice is an incredibly useful painting "tool"—or additive, actually—that adds a granular texture directly to the pigments themselves. Pumice is great when you want rough-textured fur or other grainy effects without having to rely on a textured painting surface. Pumice is readily available: you can buy a box in any hardware store (it's often used for polishing furniture). First mix the pumice with enough matte painting medium to make it fairly liquid so it will spread easily. Then add your acrylic color to the mix. If you'd like, you can also use pumice as a thickening agent to make acrylics into a paste for drier paint applications such as scumbling. For the toucan below I used gel pumice (sold at art stores) and scumbled pure paint over the texture. Try experimenting with different tools and materials, and see what different textures and effects you can create.

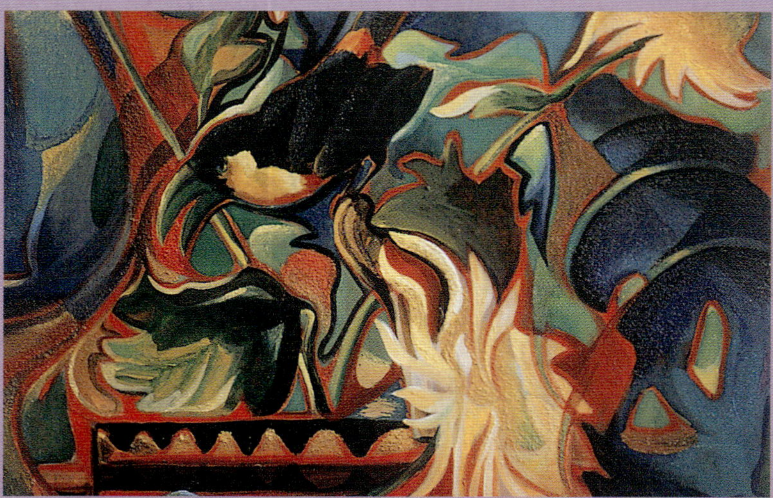

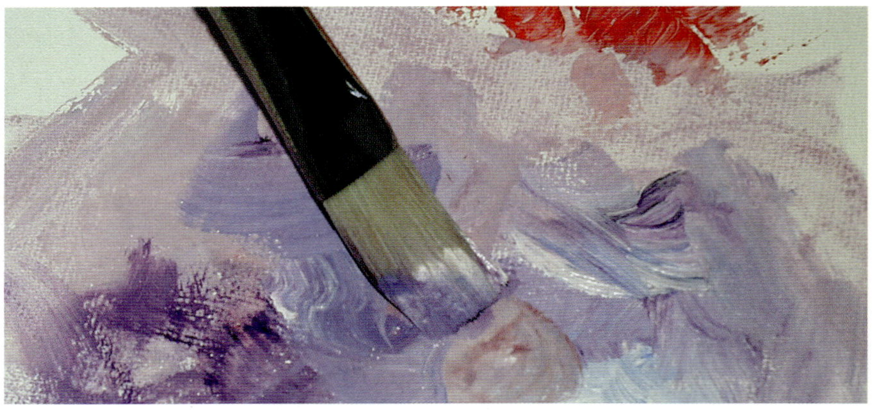

IMPASTO Applying very thick layers of paint is referred to as *impasto*. This texturizing technique creates thick edges and ridges of paint, similar to the skin of a crocodile or an alligator.

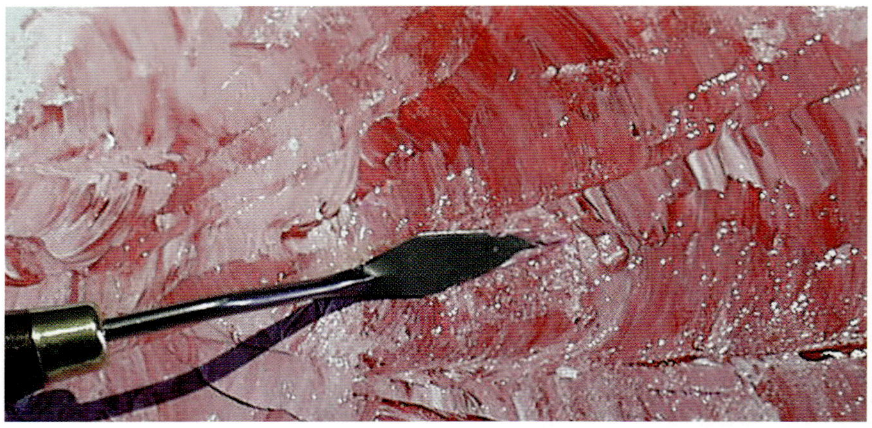

PALETTE KNIFE Another fast way to create texture is to use a palette knife. You can apply it thickly or thinly by varying the amount of pressure you use, and the texture resembles the skin of an elephant or rhino.

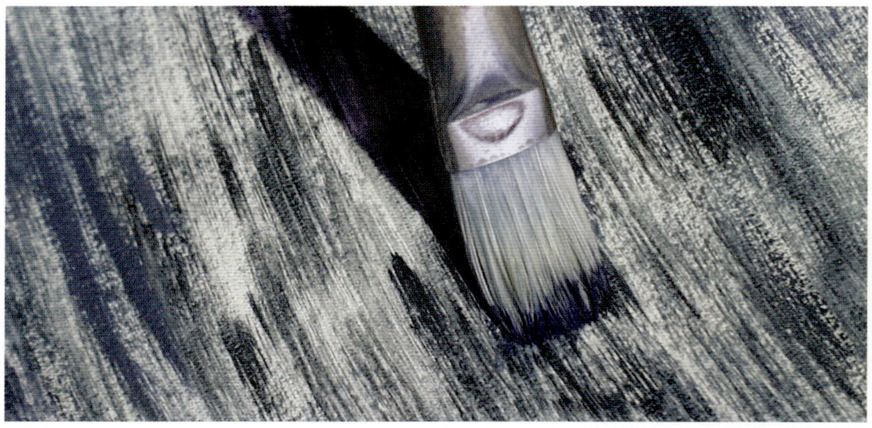

DRYBRUSHING Using a dry brush creates rough, broken strokes that resemble hair or fur. You can add a little pumice to dry your paint if you are working on canvas, board, or watercolor paper.

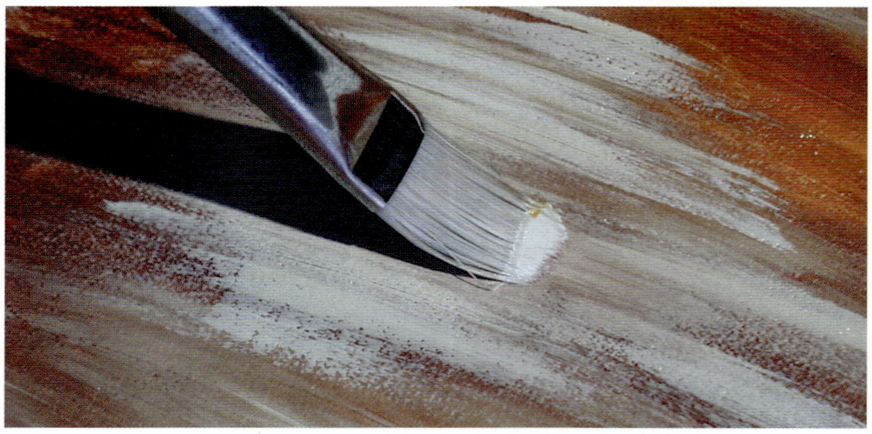

SCUMBLING This technique is good for hair or feathers. Take very dry paint and lightly drag over a drier area. (The surface must have texture so the paint can catch on the "hills" and miss the "valleys.")

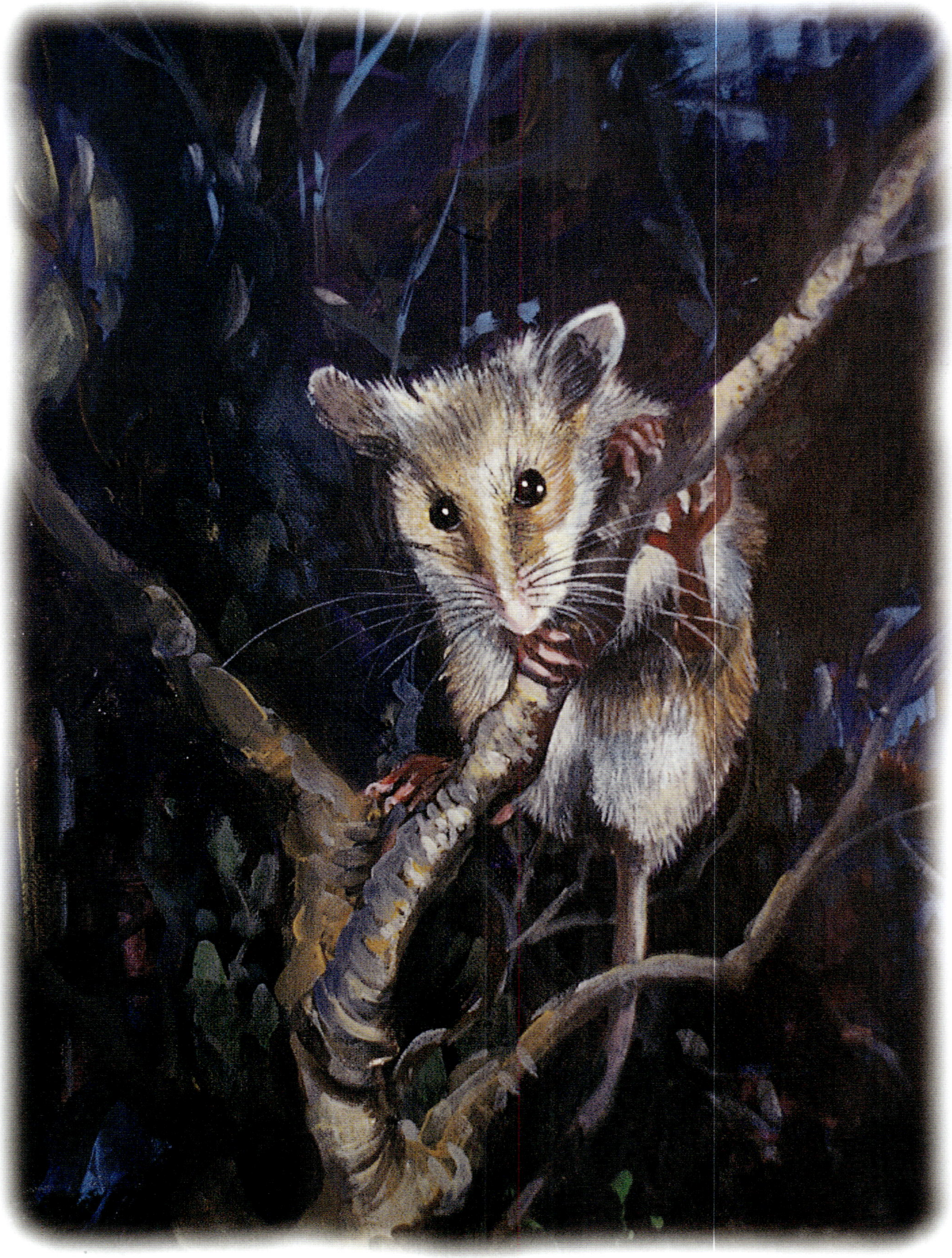

▼ **PAINTING A MOUSE** I started by blocking in the colors on the mouse and adding the darker background colors with loose strokes to provide a contrast for the fine texture of the mouse's fur.

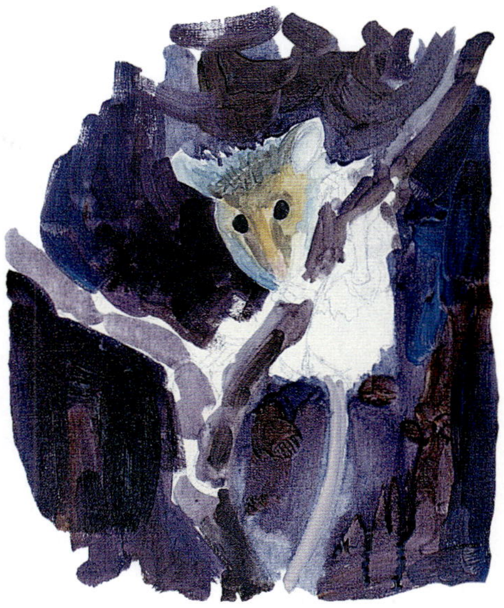

▼ **CREATING HAIR TEXTURES** To stroke on many hairs at once, I take an old brush and split hairs to separate them. (The paint can't be too wet, or the brush bristles won't stay separated.) Then I use a dry brush to apply paint, stroking in the direction of growth.

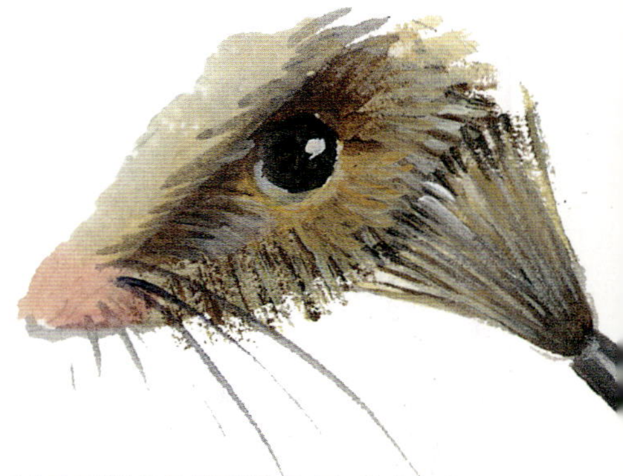

◄ **ADDING DETAILS** To finish, I painted the whiskers with a very fine pointed round and added highlights in the eyes.

► **STUDYING WILD ANIMALS** Sometimes I take a pen, pencil, watercolor paints, and half a sheet of watercolor paper and go to the zoo to study the textures, colors, and structures of various animals. I usually get quite a few good drawings to take home for future reference. For these excursions, I prefer not to use acrylics because they dry a little too fast outdoors. I also have to be able to work quickly, as the animals tend to move a lot. (Animals are usually most active in the morning, so you might want to wait until later in the day.) I don't try to get an exact likeness or fuss with details—the idea is to record quick gesture sketches of an animal's movements and salient characteristics.

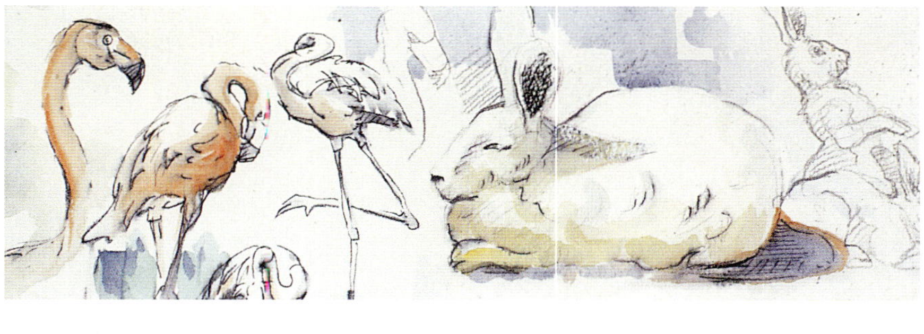

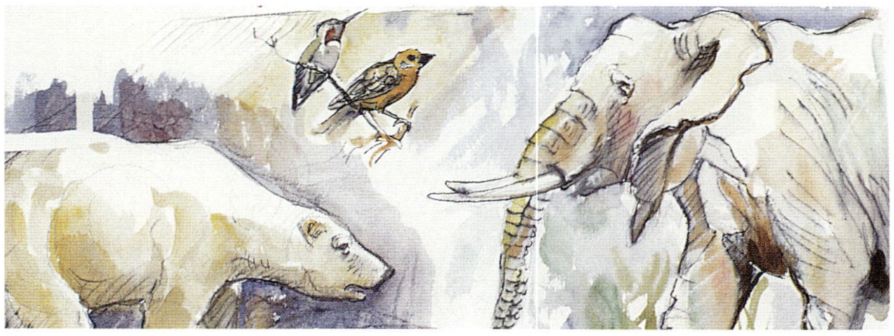

▼ **DEPICTING SCALES** Reptile skin has a distinct, repetitive design, so I started this painting with a detailed pencil drawing of the scale pattern. Next I applied a very diluted paint layer (called a *wash*) of transparent green that gave the snake volume but still allowed the pencil drawing to show through. Then I layered opaque white highlights on the top of the scales—as if they were lit by a camera's flash—and added dark lines with a fine pointed round to delineate the individual scales.

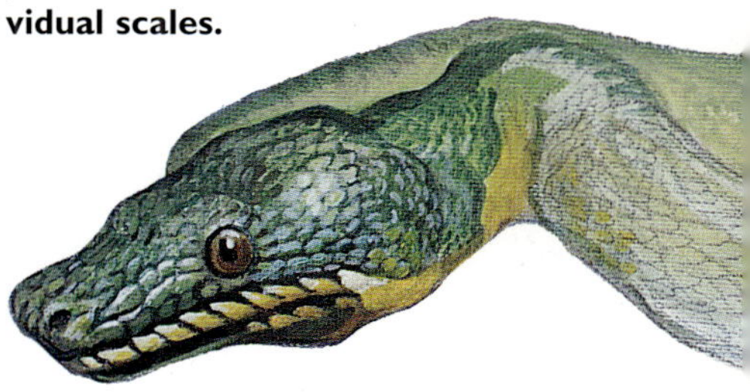

Finding a Good Focus

LANDSCAPE PAINTING is all about focus. When I paint a landscape, I take a vast panorama of infinite possibilities and squeeze it into a small picture plane—my finite painting. The least I can do to honor nature in my downsized version is to follow the few simple rules of composition that make paintings more interesting. I make sure the focal point is off-center; I situate the horizon at the top or lower third of the painting; and I place high-contrast areas of color, texture, and value against neutral areas.

Choosing a Center of Interest

I base my focal point for landscape paintings on what first catches my eye. This is what has stimulated me to paint the scene in the first place, so it makes sense that this is what the painting should focus on. I guess you could say that the focal point finds me, rather than the other way around! For example, in the painting below, I was attracted by the interesting lines of the pier and the stark contrast of the white house against the deep blue sky. To get the best possible focus, I used my fingers as a viewfinder (see box at right) and surveyed the scene from different angles until I had both the house and the pier in view. Then I placed the house to the left of center, using the lines of the pier to attract the viewer's eye and guide it to the bright, white house.

Finding the Best View

The best way to find a good focal point and to make sure you have an interesting composition is to look through a viewfinder. You can buy a simple viewfinder, but I think the most convenient viewfinder is one formed by your own fingers, as shown below.

On both hands, make an "L" with your first and second finger, then turn one hand over and hold them together as shown, slightly overlapping your fingers and thumbs. Slide each "L" to make the opening rectangular or square, and look through the opening at the scene you'd like to paint. Move this viewfinder around to survey the scene from several different angles until you find one that suits you. The advantage of this "handy" viewfinder is that you can match a composition to the vertical or horizontal format of your paper by sliding your fingers into a vertical or horizontal format. And you'll never misplace this viewfinder!

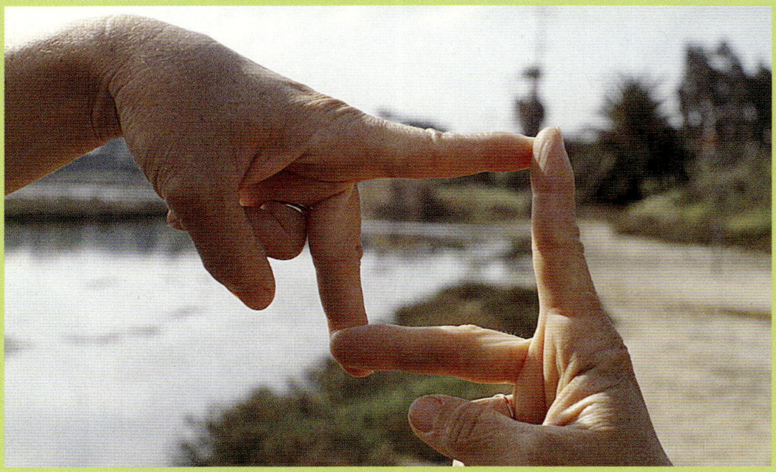

Choosing the Format

Once I've chosen a focal point and a viewpoint, I need to decide which format, or shape, would be best for the painting. The format you use will primarily depend on the size and shape of your subject, but not entirely. To a certain degree, you can choose a format that will emphasize certain aspects of your subject for greater impact. Compare the three pictures shown here to see the difference format can make in a painting.

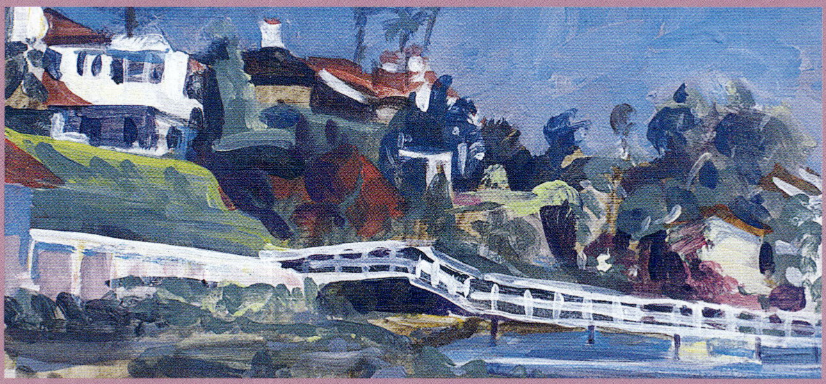

◄ EMPHASIZING THE HORIZON This wide format is perfect for a panoramic scene such as this one. This narrow format would also be good for a landscape or seascape painting, where you want to accentuate a wide expanse of land, sky, or water.

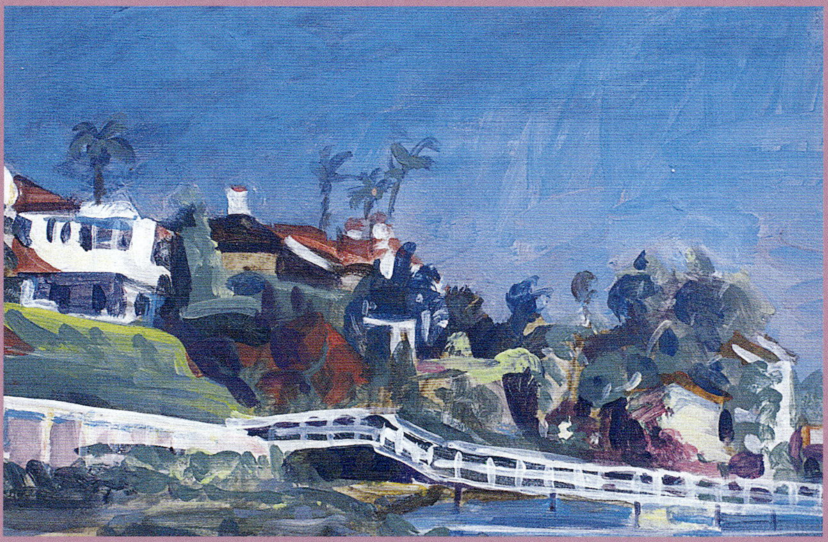

► ENCOMPASSING THE WHOLE The traditional landscape format is the horizontal rectangle. In this format, which is similar to the one above but not quite so extreme, I could show both the house and the pier, yet still have enough space above to include more of the sky. This created interesting contrasts between the relatively flat sky and the more detailed foreground.

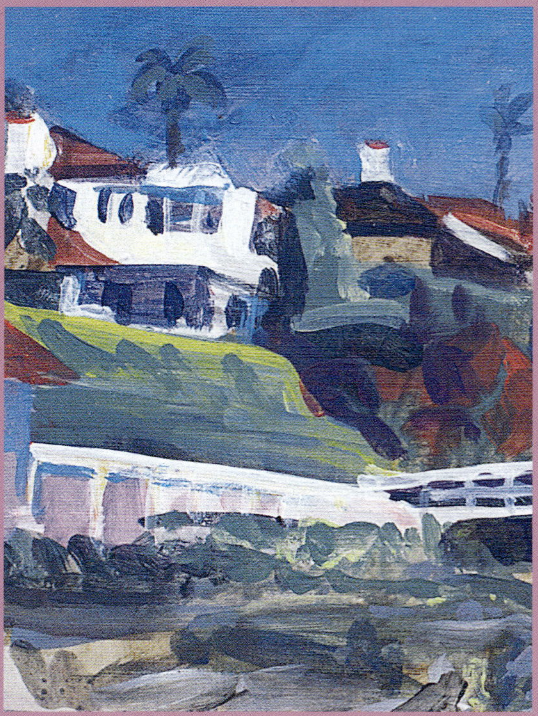

▲ CONVEYING HEIGHT Here I placed the same scene as the one above in a vertical format to focus on the house and to emphasize the sheerness of the cliff. This format would also be suitable for tall subjects—a person standing or a vase of flowers, perhaps—or when you want to exaggerate height for a more dramatic effect.

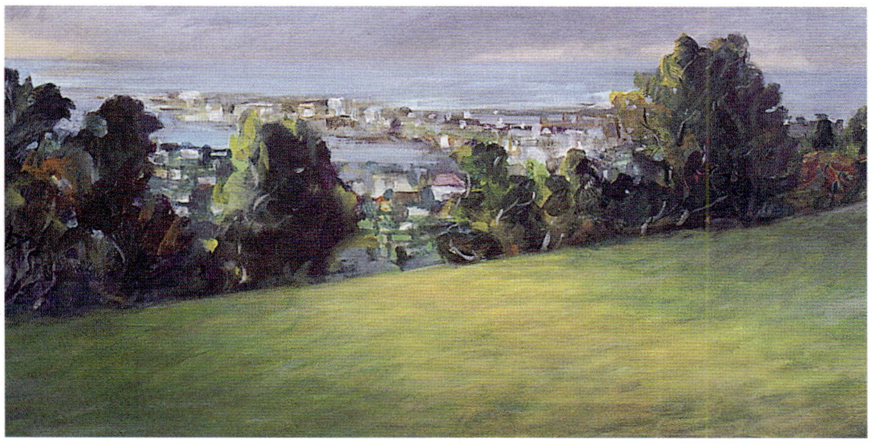

◂ SETTING A HIGH HORIZON LINE This composition divides the subject horizontally into thirds. Because the horizon is set on the upper third, I had to make sure the middle ground and especially the foreground were interesting. The focal point is where the dark trees on the left contrast with the bright glow on the grass, while the details fade toward the right.

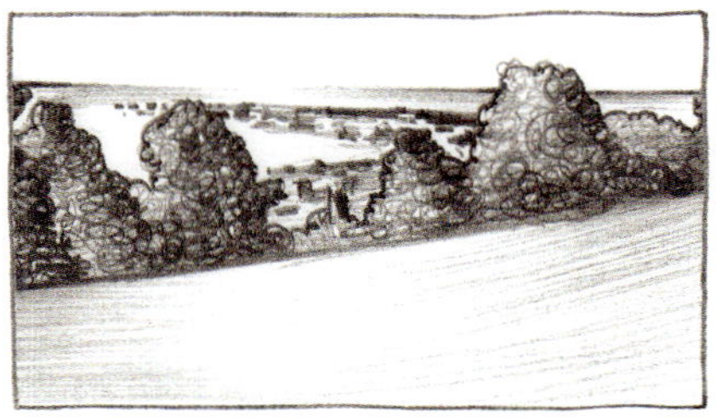

Good format: High horizon

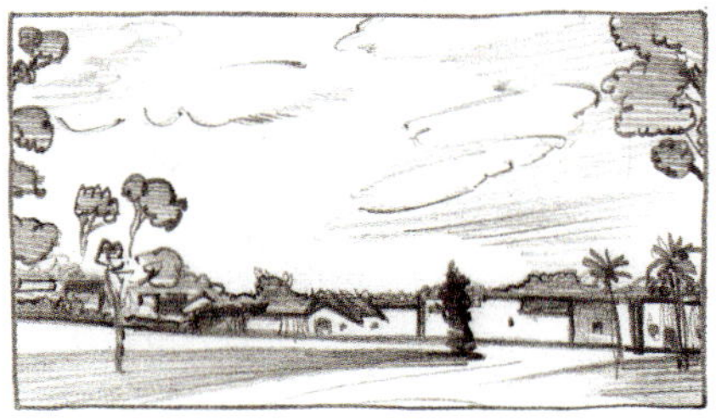

Good format: Low horizon

▸ SETTING A LOW HORIZON LINE When the horizon line is low, the large sky can act as a passive space to highlight something going on below, or the sky itself can be the center of interest. In this scene, the field and busy row of houses are the focal point, so I placed a diagonal path in the foreground to lead the eye right to the area of interest.

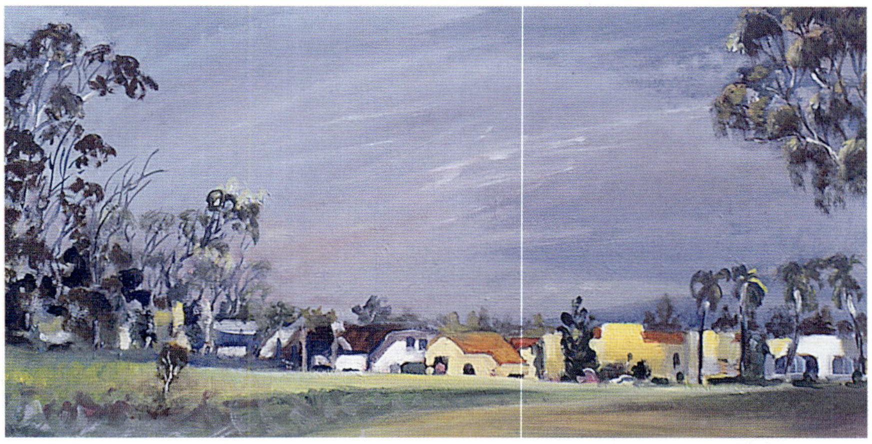

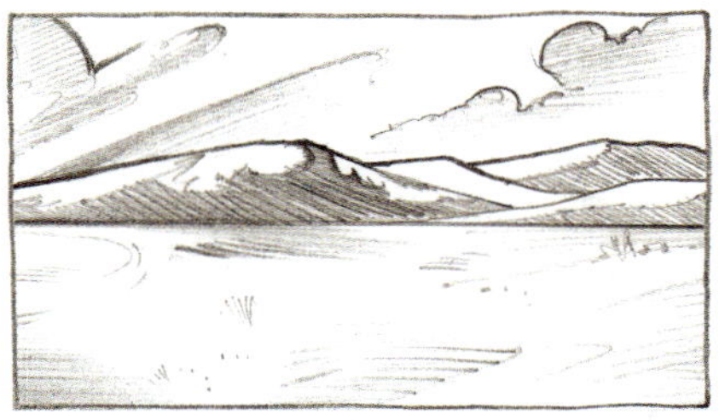

Bad format: Centered horizon

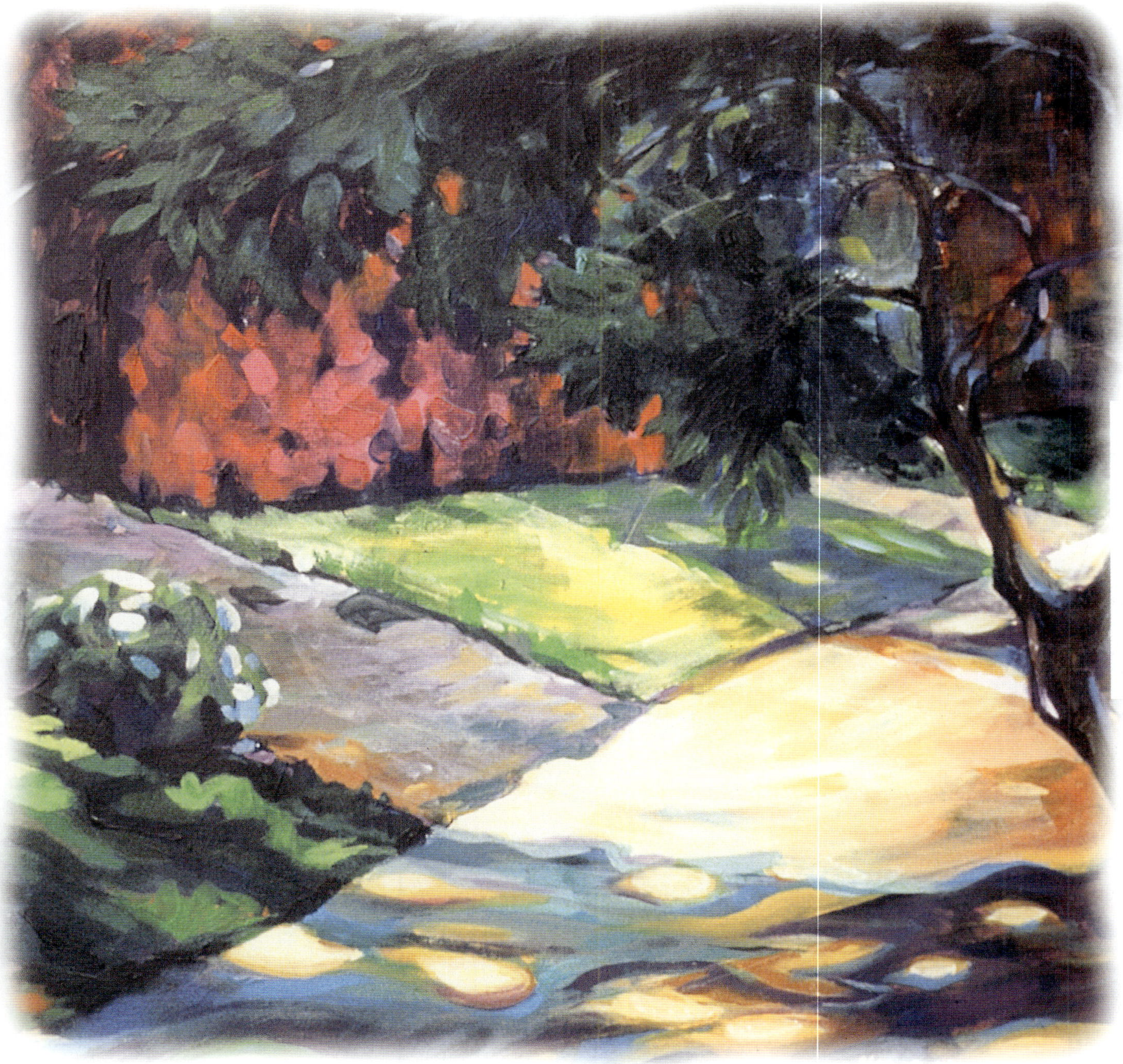

◂ FRAMING A HIGH-INTEREST AREA In this composition, I chose a bright spot of bougainvillea and used extreme lights and darks for the areas that stimulate the eye. Most of this painting was done with a palette knife, which really allowed me to pile on the paint and create an effective texture—especially on the sun-dappled pathway.

Artist's Tip

Be aware that if you put people in a landscape painting, they may automatically become the focal point because the eye is drawn first to whatever is different in a scene.

Looking at Waves and Water

MANY CHARACTERISTICS OF WATER are fascinating to me, and many books have been written on how to paint reflections and such. Here I'd like to focus on the ocean—and, in particular, the movement of ocean swells, the color of waves, and how to paint underwater scenes. Acrylic's ability to be both opaque and transparent makes it wonderfully suited to painting scenes both above and below the water.

Painting an Underwater Scene

If you've ever gone scuba diving—or even seen a diver on film—you know that the water gets darker the farther down you go. However, the ocean does not just get darker; it actually changes color. Nearer to the surface, where some sunlight penetrates the water, you can see more yellows and reds in sea creatures and other objects, and the color of the water is lighter and more yellow. As you go deeper, the color becomes bluer and darker; at the deepest levels there are shades of green, blue-green, blue, blue-gray, and black.

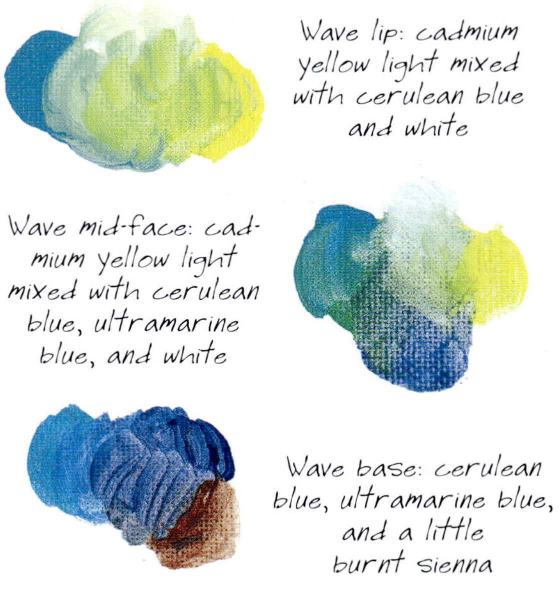

WAVE COLORS Waves have three distinct color areas: the lip, the mid-face, and the base. Above I have shown the color mixes I used for the wave in the painting at right.

Capturing a Wave

The color of a wave changes during the day as the light changes. On a noontime wave, there is a translucence on the thin lip that reflects down onto the center of the wave (see the study below). In the early morning or at dusk, when there is no direct sunlight, there is no translucency either—everything is more muted in color.

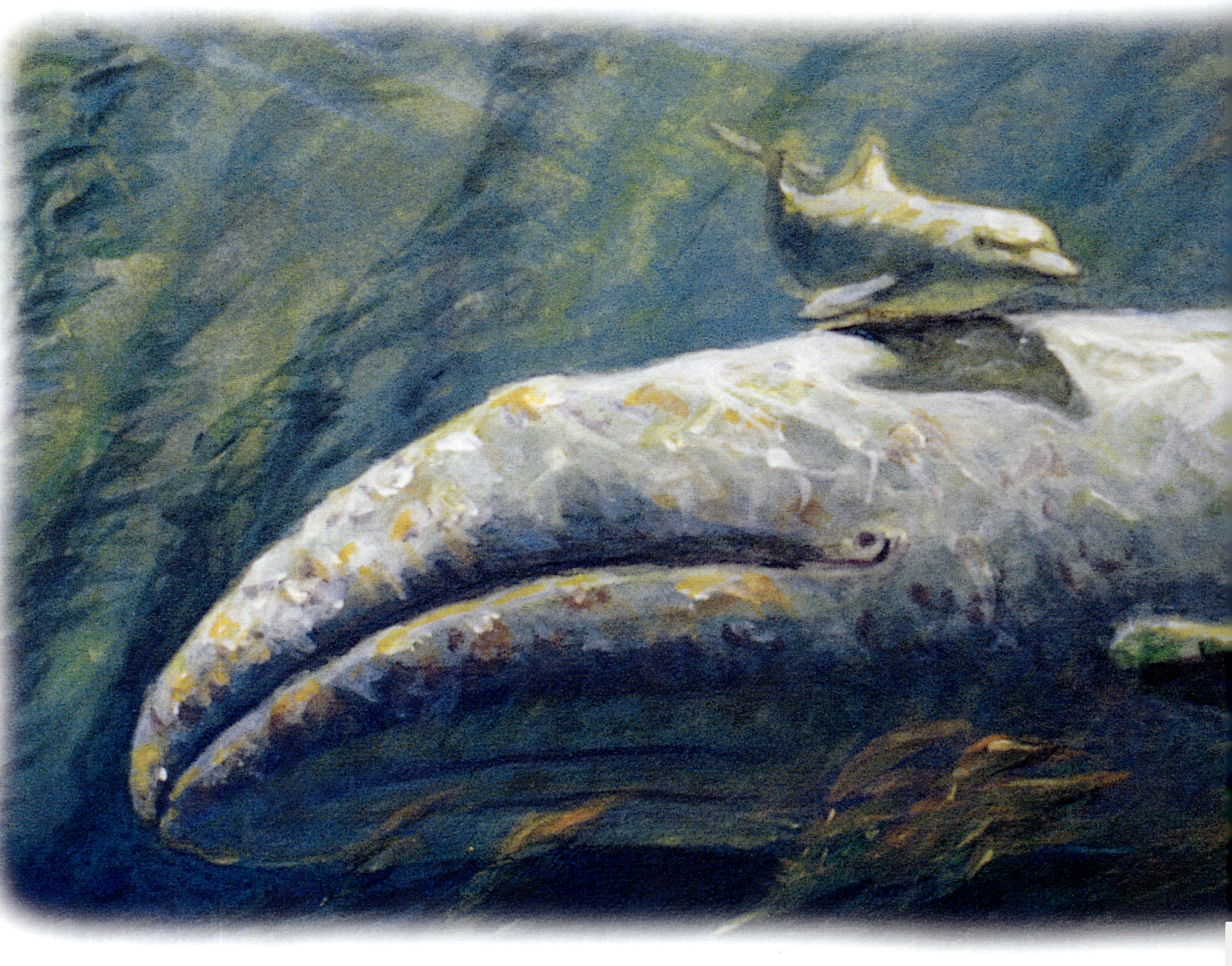

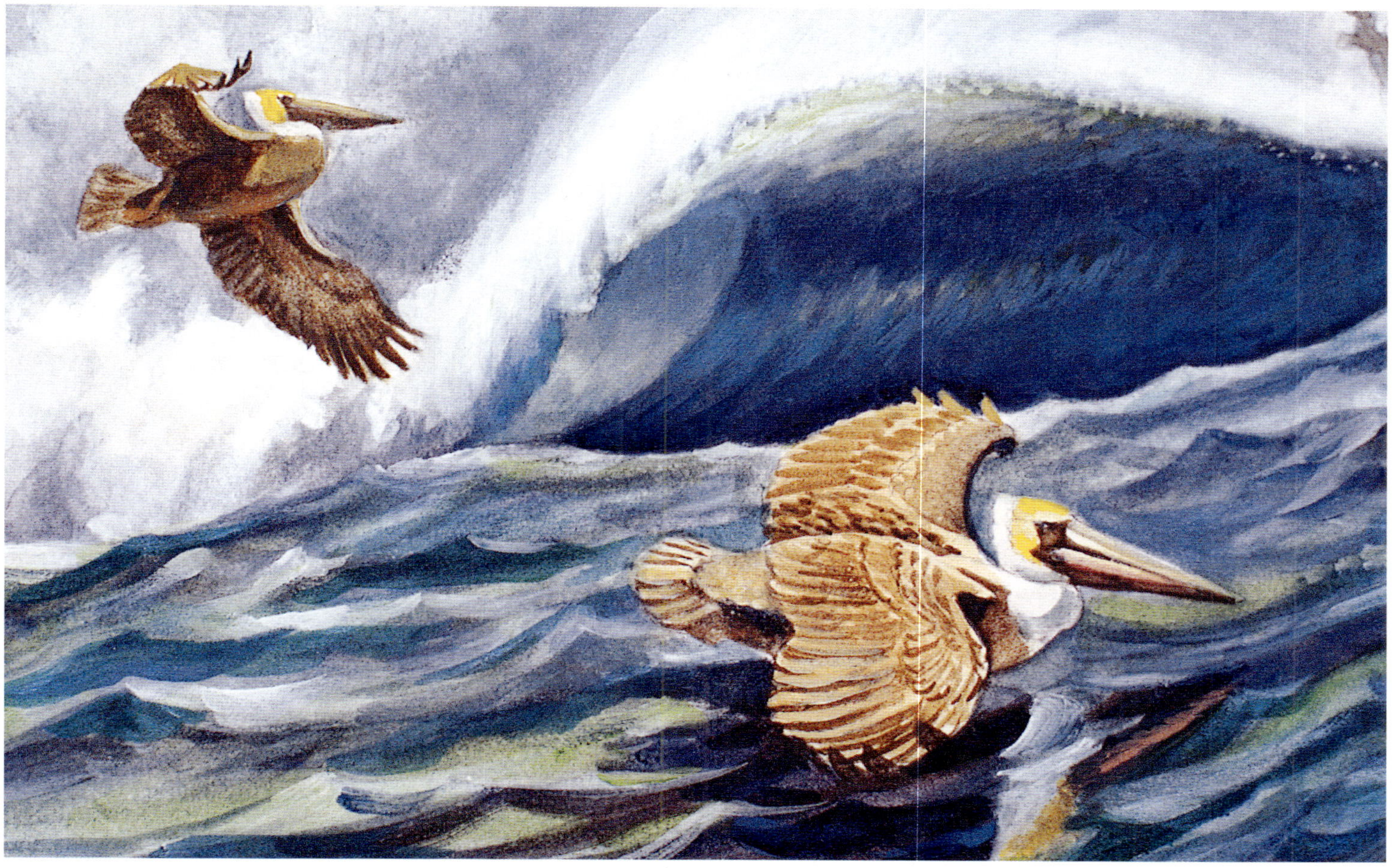

◂ BUILDING UP COLOR This painting was begun with thin, watercolor-like washes of blues and greens. As I proceeded, I began to use more white for the light areas and more opaque colors in the water and the sea birds. For the wave, I used the colors listed for the samples on page 12.

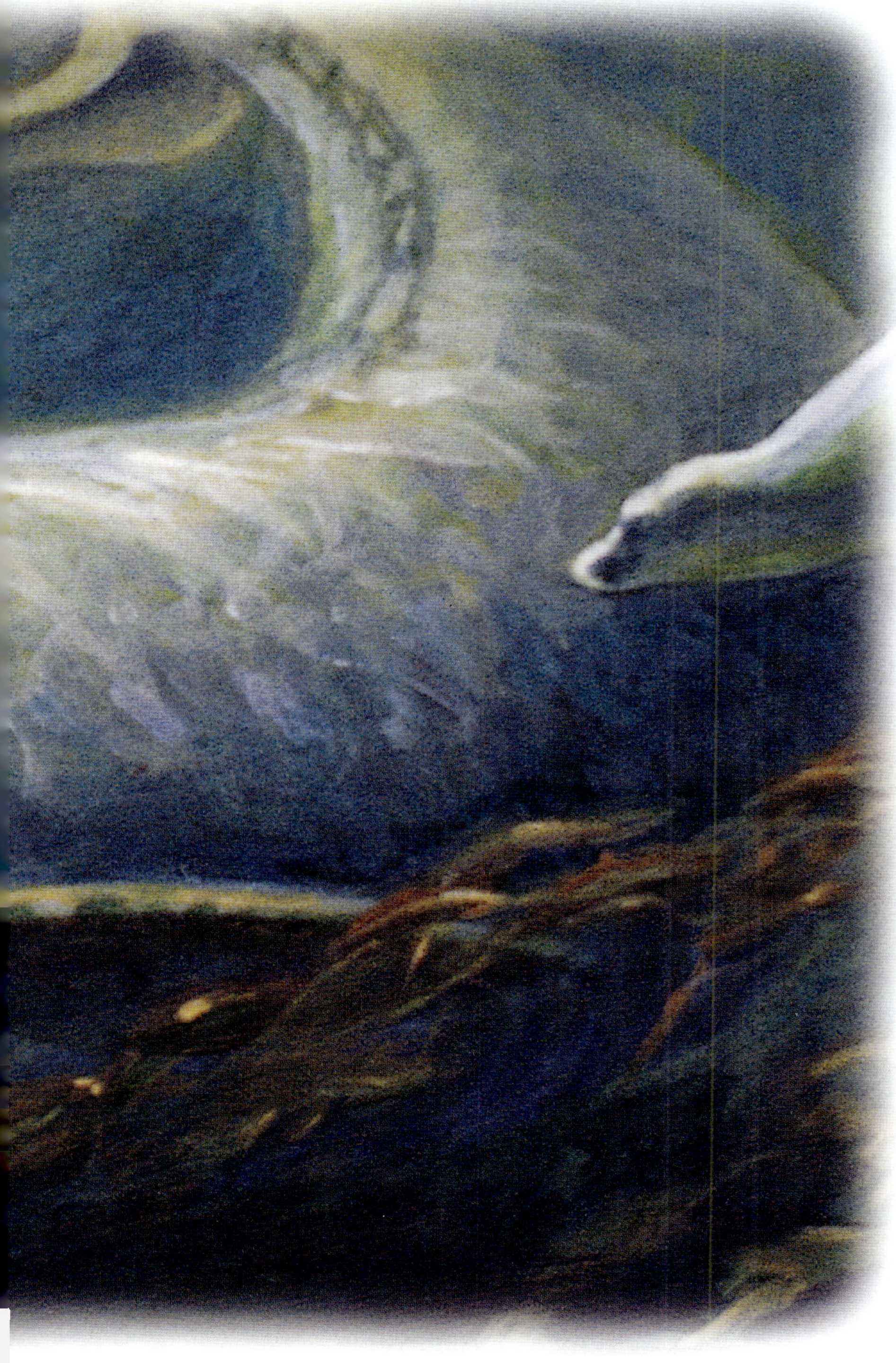

◂ BELOW THE SURFACE Working from a photo, I started this painting on a fairly dark yellow-green surface, sketching the animals in with pencil. After I had painted the mottled light patterns and other details on the whale, I glazed over them with a wash of transparent light blue. This served to push the animals and kelp back into the bluish atmosphere. I finished with a few white dappled highlights.

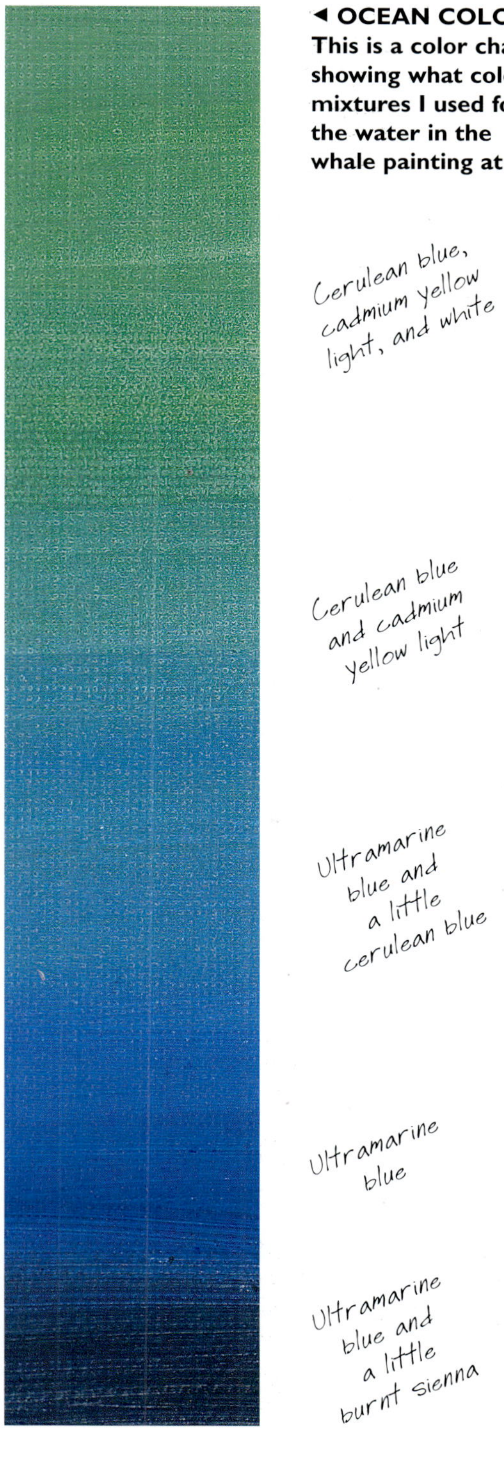

◂ OCEAN COLORS This is a color chart showing what color mixtures I used for the water in the whale painting at left.

The Power of Neutrals

ACRYLIC IS KNOWN for its vivid colors, but did you know that the secret to making brilliant colors look truly beautiful is using neutrals to set them off? Neutrals (basically browns and grays) are the "strong, silent partners" in a painting, allowing the brighter colors to really stand out, and you can create them easily by mixing various colors on your palette. You may not have thought much about neutrals before, but a painting that utilizes a range of neutrals can be just as effective as one bustling with vibrant colors, and it conveys a quieter mood.

Focusing on Neutrals

When beginning to paint, your first instinct may be to use all the beautiful bright, pure colors on your palette and to try hard not to "muddy" them. But the world is full of wonderful nuances of grays and browns that have a richness of color of their own. If you look carefully, you'll see that what at first appears to be gray is really violet or that a brown field is a mix of reds and greens. Look at the chart below, and practice mixing a variety of colors to see the range of neutrals you can produce. You'll find that your neutral mixes will have more complexity and "life" than any brown or gray found in a tube.

MIXING NEUTRALS This chart shows a few neutral colors and how to create them by mixing the three primary colors (red, yellow, and blue) or by mixing complements—colors opposite each other on the color wheel (red and green, yellow and purple, blue and orange). Notice the color variations of neutrals you can create, from reddish-brown to purplish-gray, depending on the colors you use and which ones dominate.

Mixing with Primaries

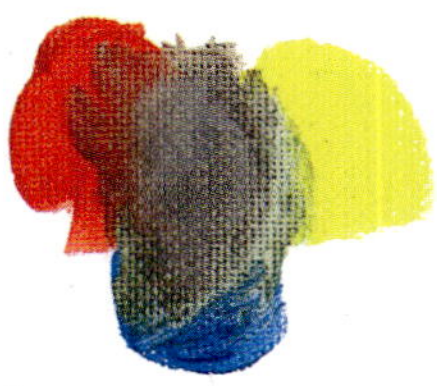

All three primaries mixed in equal parts (a basic neutral)

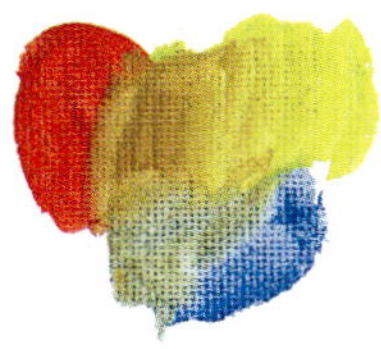

All three primaries mixed with extra cadmium yellow

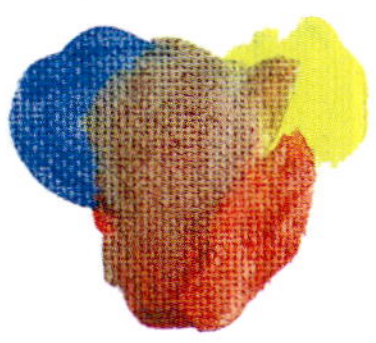

All three primaries mixed with extra cadmium red

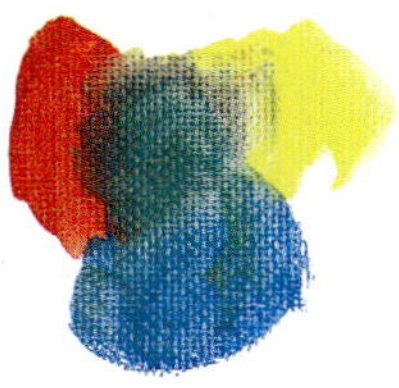

All three primaries mixed with extra cobalt blue

Mixing with Complements

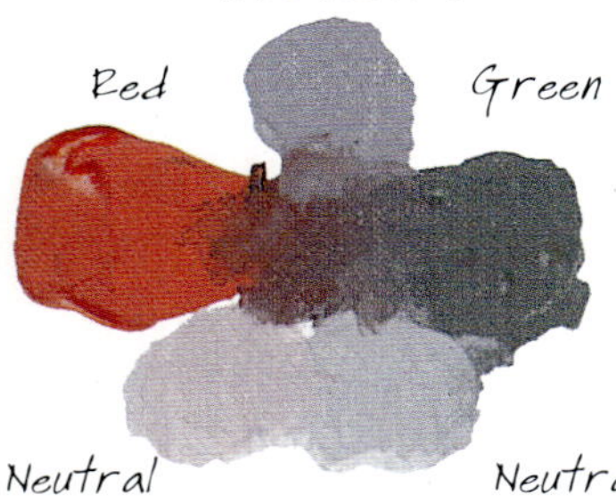

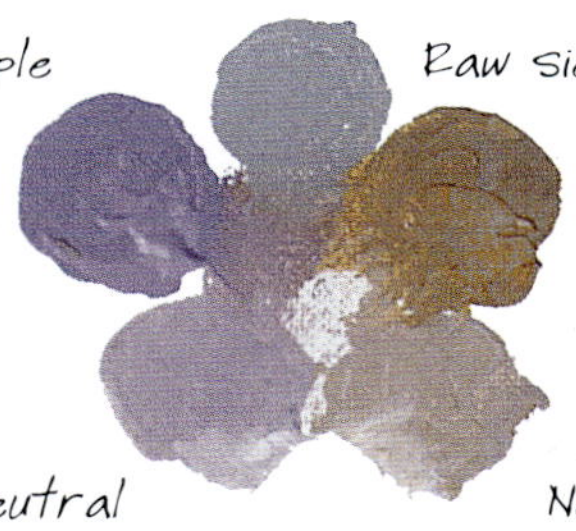

Painting with Complements

Mixing complements creates neutral grays and browns. But placing complements next to each other has the opposite effect: they add a sense of liveliness and vibrancy. Here the bold use of the complements orange and blue give this painting energy and make the subject really "pop!"

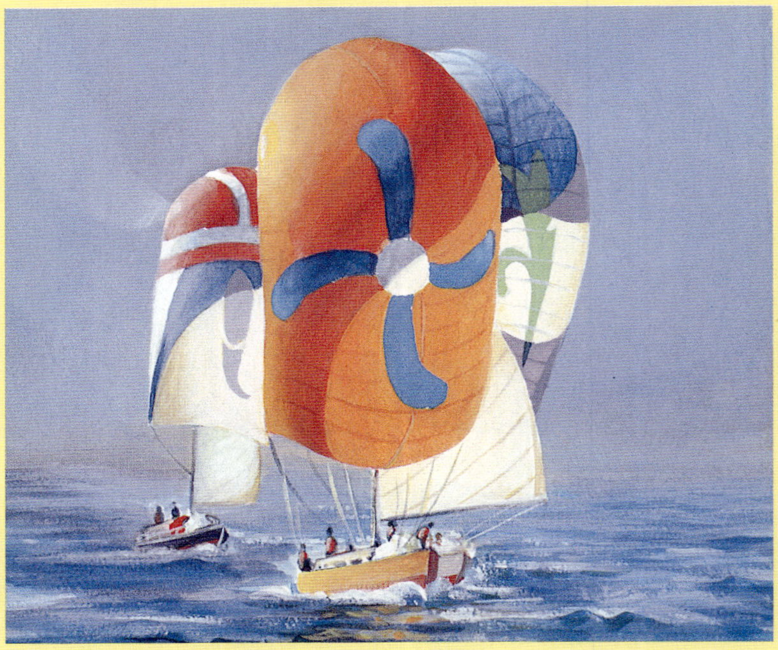

Using Neutrals to Create Mood

Have you ever noticed that certain paintings seem serene and quiet, whereas others seem active and loud? That is because colors arouse emotional responses, and soft neutrals are calm and peaceful, while bright colors are bold and exciting. Compare the painting in the box above with the ones on the opposite page, and consider the different feelings each evokes. Then use the power of neutrals to your advantage in your paintings, letting them dominate when you want to convey tranquility and using them sparingly when you want your painting to shout!

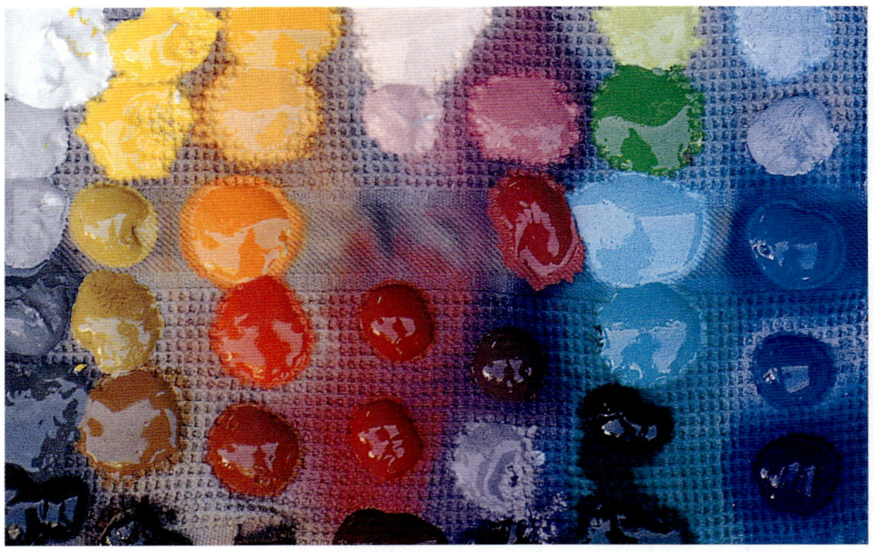

ARRANGING THE PALETTE Here is the way I lay out my colors to make mixing neutrals easier. On the left side of the palette, I place five neutrals, ranging from light to dark, plus white and black. To their right, I place my pure colors, lining up with the neutrals from light to dark. To neutralize a pure color, I just pull it out and mix it with a nearby neutral, adding more or less of each color until I have the neutral I want.

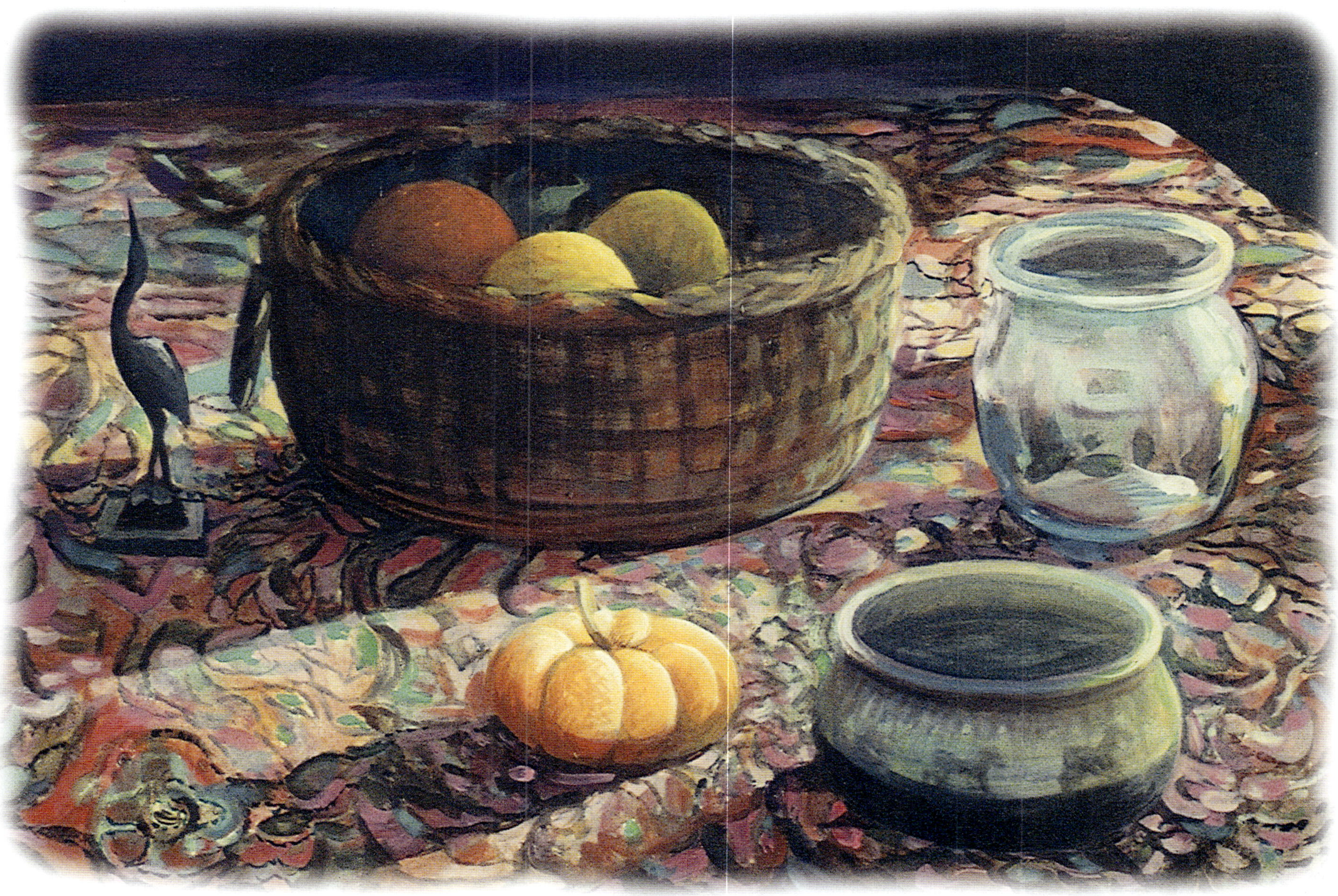

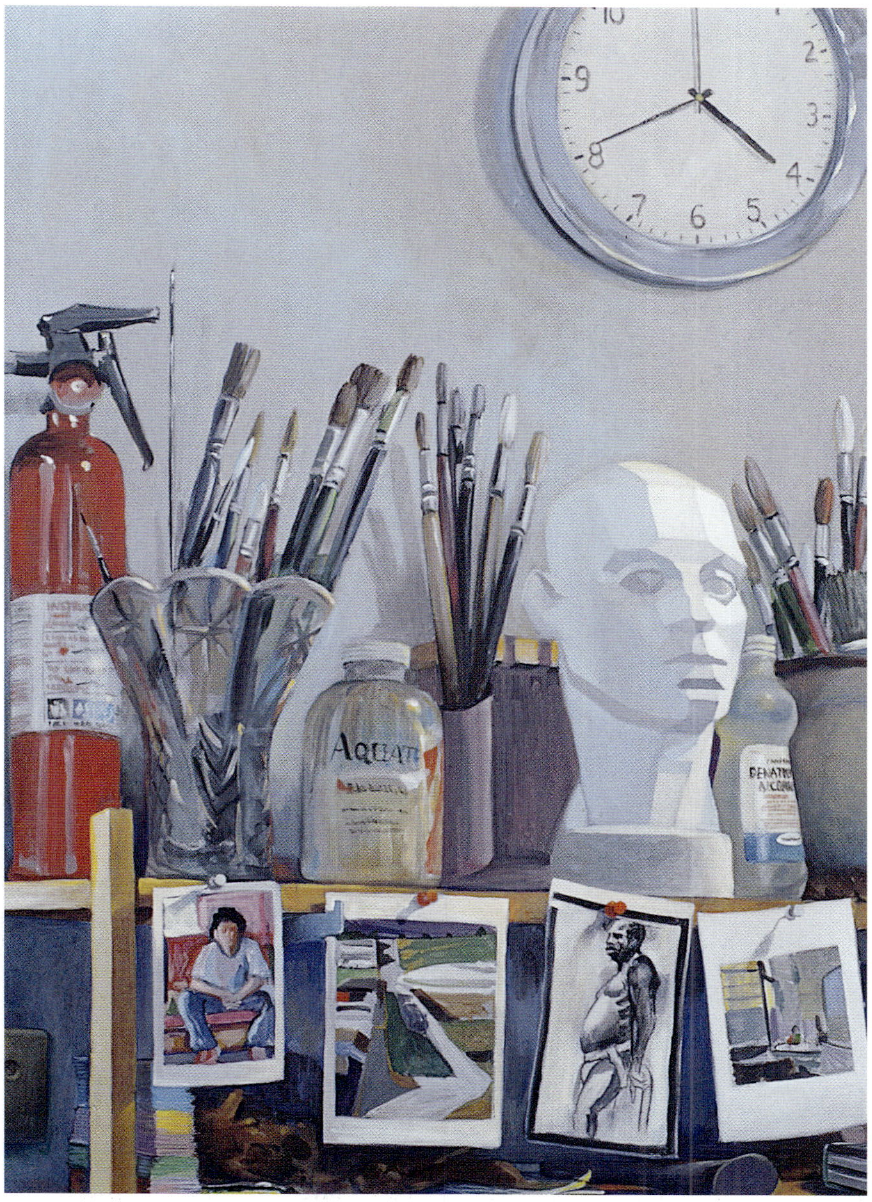

▲ ACCENTING WARM BROWN NEUTRALS Compare this still life with *Fire Extinguisher* (below left), which has a passive gray background and small, busy shapes. In this painting everything is relatively neutral and basically warm brown, except for the cool colors of the two bowls, the glass egg, and the few accents of turquoise. Notice how even subtle color differences make these items stand out amid the browns.

Planning Your Color Scheme

When you plan what colors to use for a painting, think about how neutrals and complements convey emotion and try to match the color scheme to your subject. For the still life above, I wanted to evoke the warm, peaceful feeling of early morning, so I chose an overall neutral brown theme and used brighter colors for accents. For the painting of my studio at left, I wanted a cool, clean, feeling of stillness, so I used a lot of blue, purple-gray, and white to contrast with the bright red fire extinguisher. Planning your color palette before you begin to paint will save you the time and trouble of correcting it later and will help to ensure a successful painting.

◄ USING COOL GRAY NEUTRALS This is primarily a painting of cool neutrality, but notice how this dominance of gray brings out the warm tones in the shelves, containers, postcards, and (especially!) the red fire extinguisher.

Artist's Tip

Acrylics look darker when dry than they do when wet! Make some test swatches and let them dry first so you'll know how to adjust your colors as you paint.

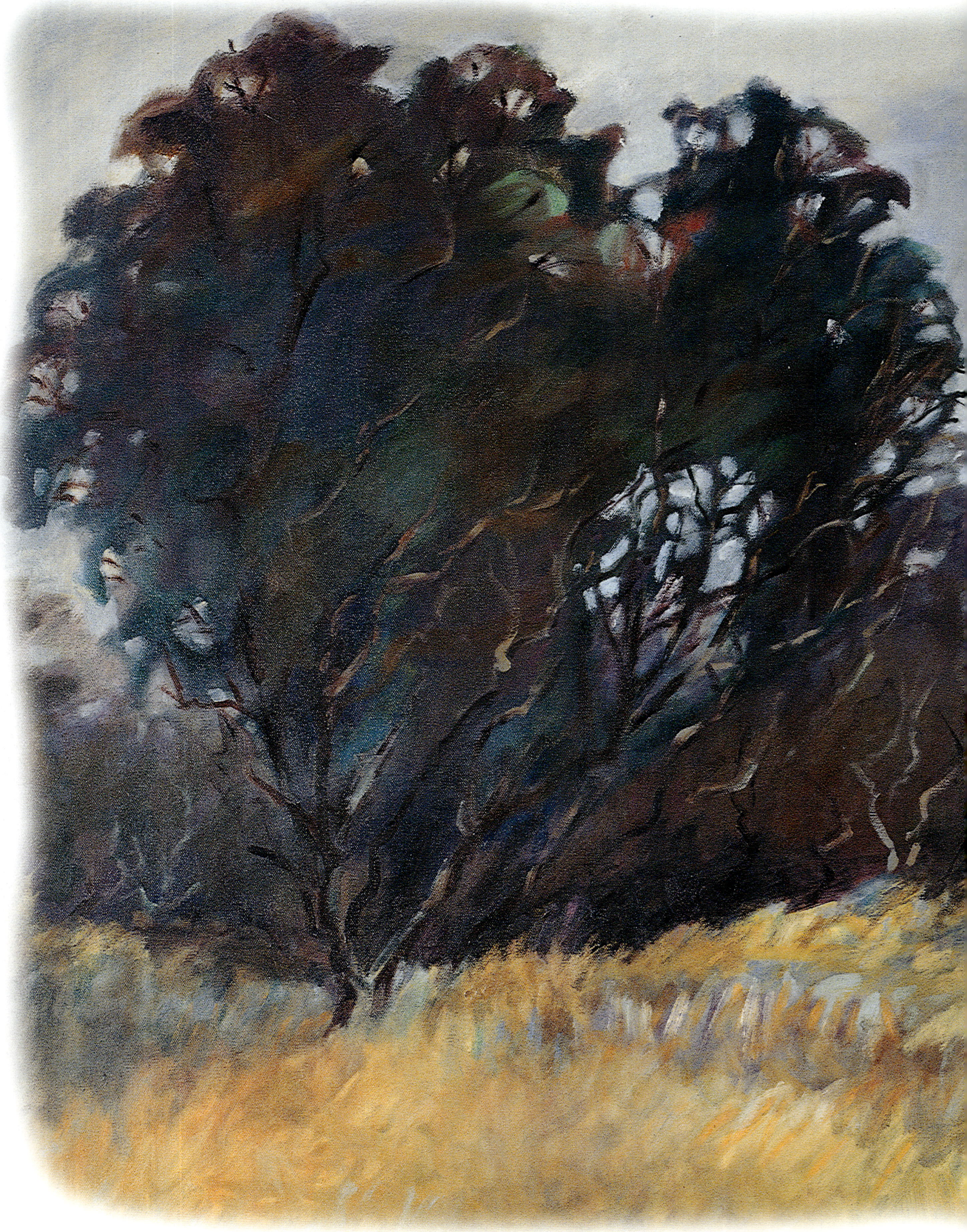

EXPRESSING NATURE'S BEAUTY The scene is simple—trees, long grass, and sky—yet there is always something new and vibrant you can bring to your

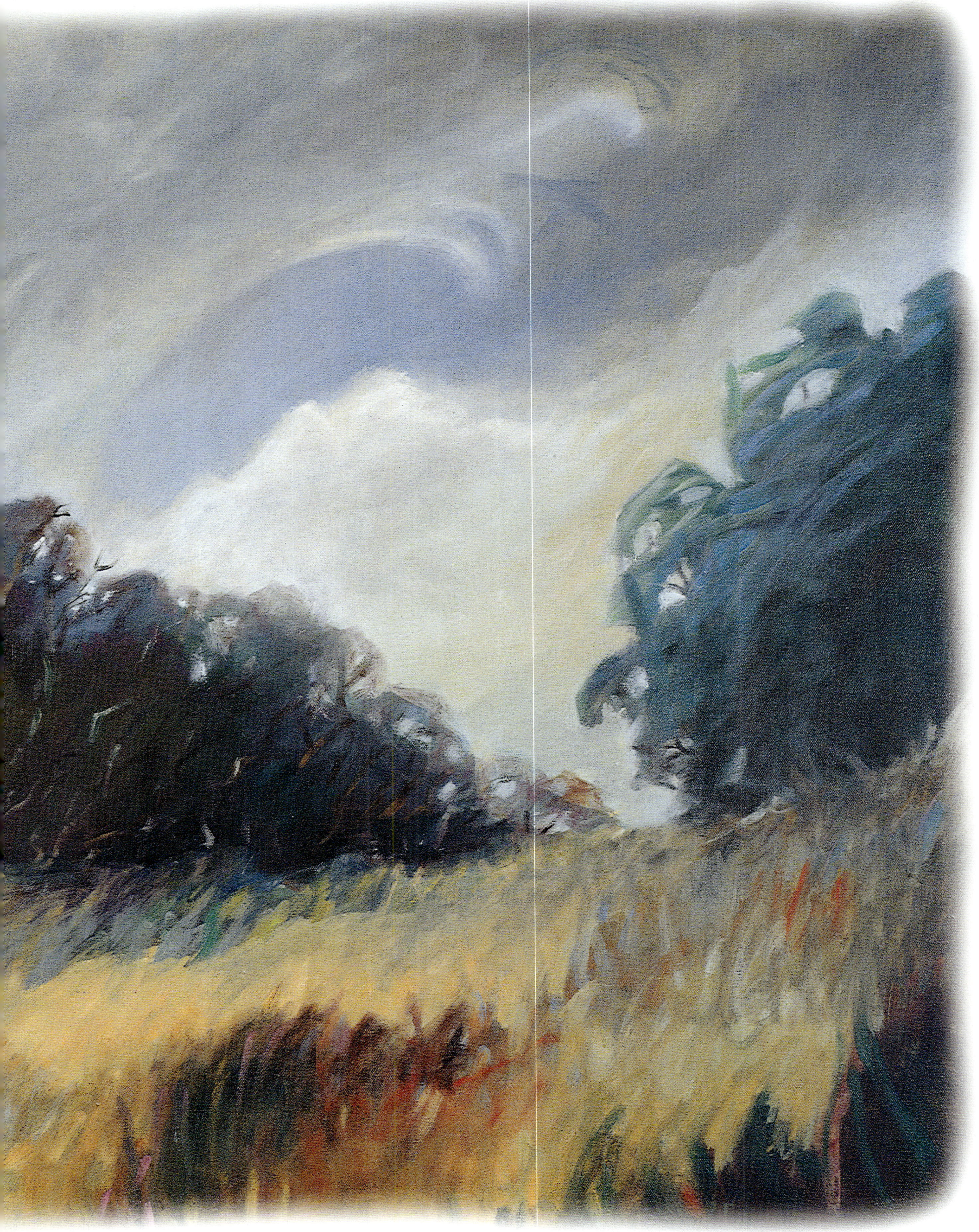

gs. This is a good example of the vibrant colors and effects you can achieve in acrylic—no matter what the subject!

Capturing Motion

MOVEMENT IN A PAINTING can mean many different things. It can refer to the way you direct the viewer's eye through a composition, or it can mean showing a figure or an animal "frozen" in mid-move. It can also relate to the way blurred brushwork is used to indicate a speeding object, or the way wavy lines show that the subject is being blown by the wind. Instead of focusing on just one type of movement, I thought it would be fun to explore a few different acrylic techniques for showing subjects in action.

Expressing Movement with Line

What image comes to mind when you think of a windy day? I think of trees bending and branches stretching out, hair blowing in streams, fabric billowing in undulating waves, and water cresting into myriad whitecaps. These are all examples of how curving lines can create the illusion of movement in objects that have some fluidity. Below I've shown the steps I took to create the illusion of flags flapping in the breeze by focusing on flowing lines and developing highlights and shadows. Notice that all the patterns on the flags follow the contours of the cylindrical-shaped folds and reinforce the line of movement. This helps integrate the stars and stripes into the fabric and keeps them from looking as if they were pasted on.

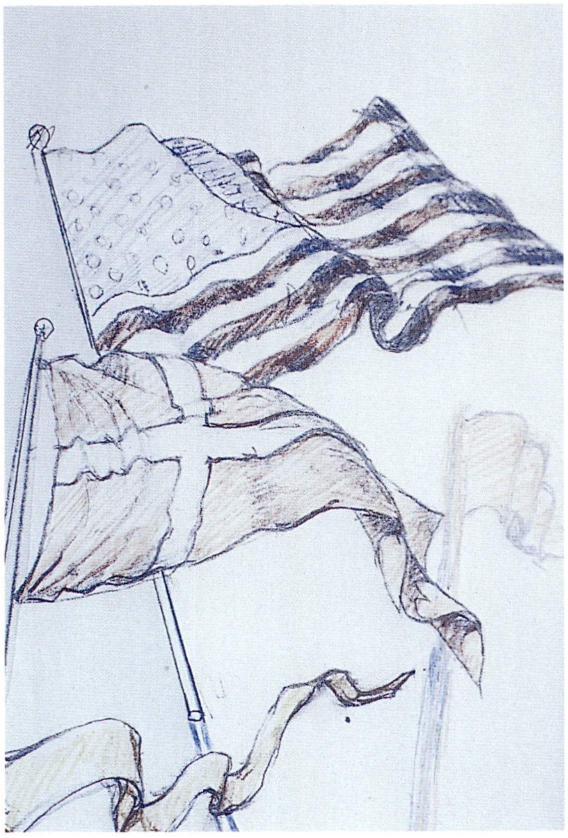

1 USING CURVED LINES I started the flags with pencil and colored pencil so I could work out the basic lines, forms, and colors before applying the acrylic. I especially wanted to make sure I had all the curved lines correct before I started rendering the forms. I drew each flag pole at a different angle since diagonals increase movement.

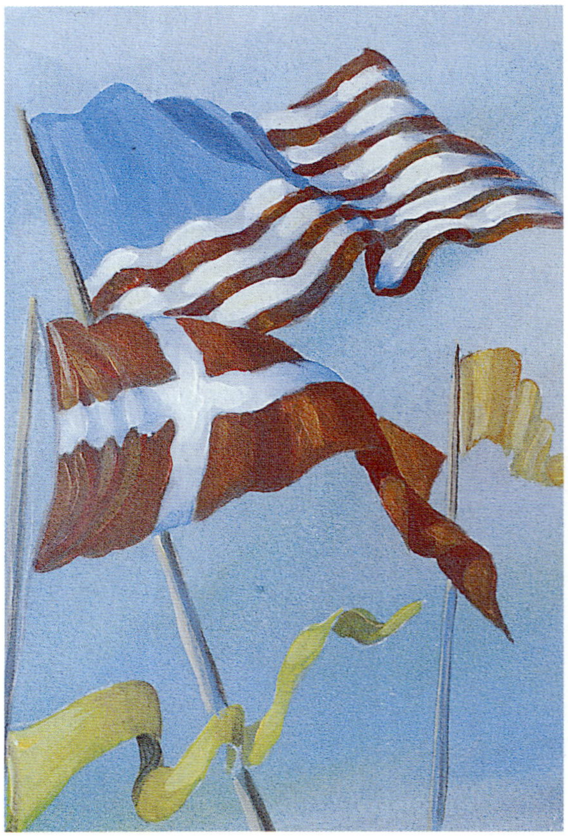

2 APPLYING COLOR I used watercolor paper and a fairly dry brush, because drier paint smudges easily and shows the texture of the paper. I like the way the blurred color adds to the feeling of movement. At this stage, I'm not concerned with details; all I'm interested in is getting the basic forms correct.

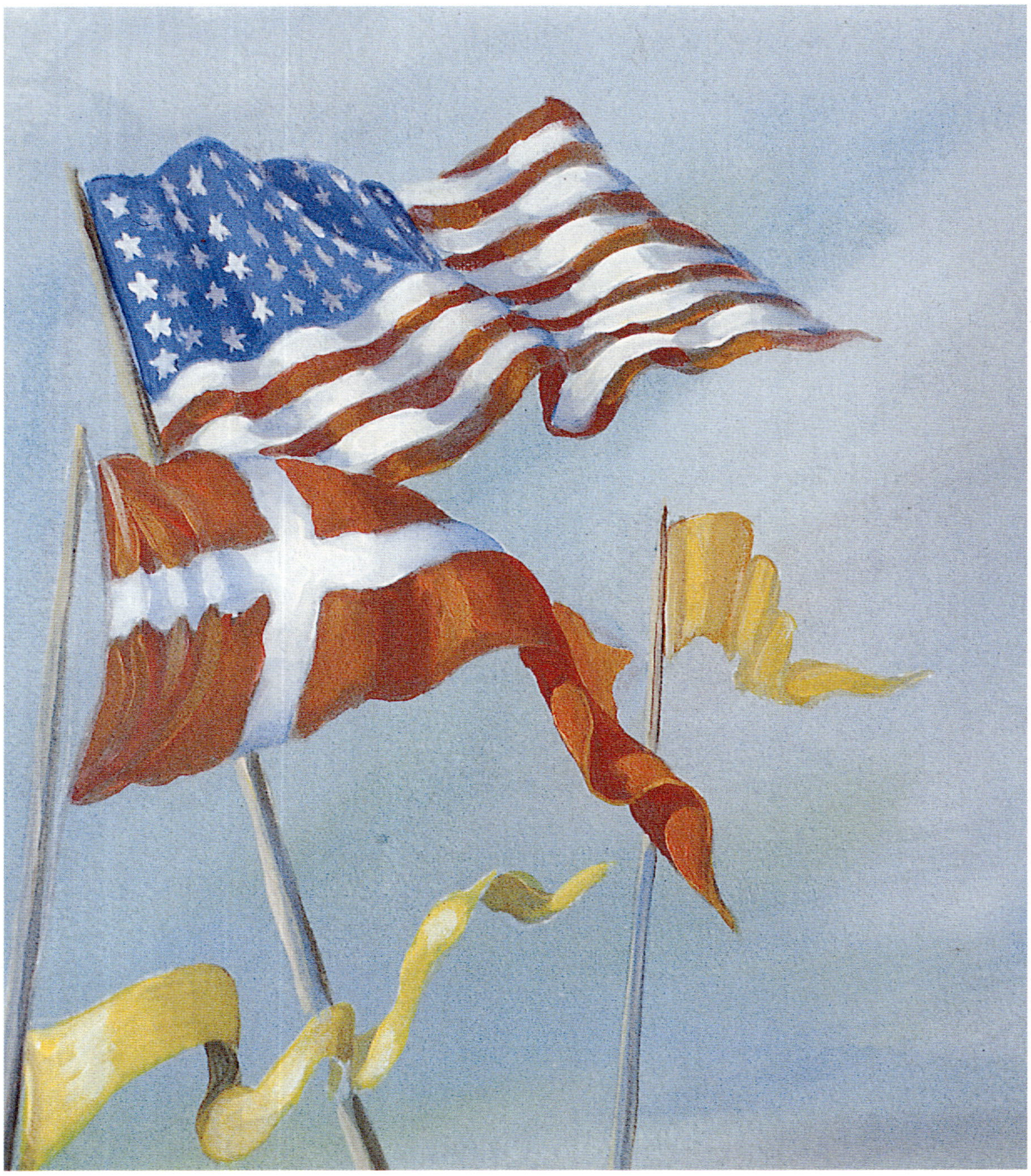

3 FINISHING FLAGS To complete this picture, I darkened the shadow areas and lightened the highlights. Then I placed stars on the American flag and finished modeling the ribbon-like forms of the other flags. Notice that the flags extend out of the picture plane, as though the paper cannot contain their movements.

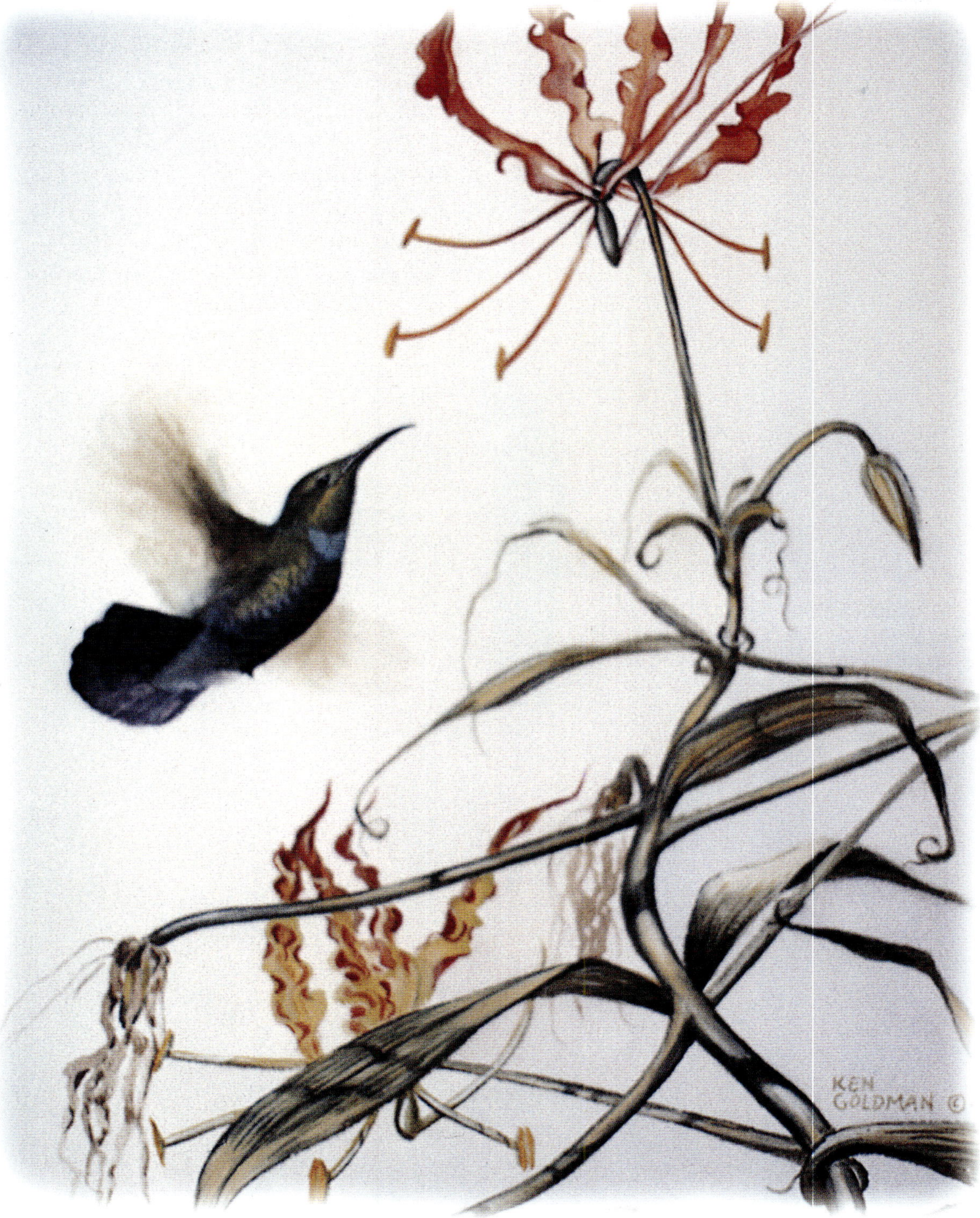

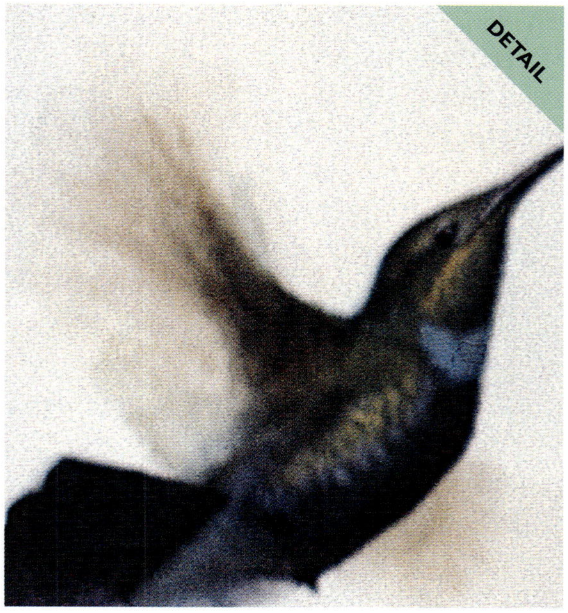

▲ **FOCUSING ON WINGS** In this detail, you can see how I blurred the wings, using drybrush and a rag. This is exactly the way they appeared to me.

Artist's Tip

I find it easier to convey a sense of movement in a painting if I work from life or sketches, rather than from photographs.

◄ **BLURRING MOVEMENT** While in Barbados, I painted this green-throated carib from life, using only binoculars and a field guide. I have always been disappointed by paintings that stop the action of hummingbird wings. Stop-action should be left to strobe cameras.

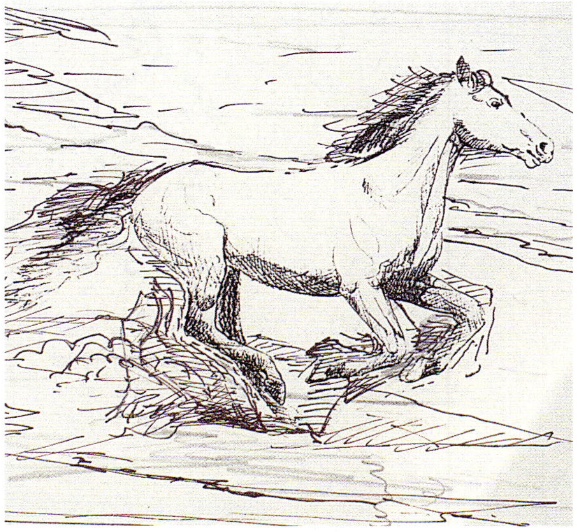

WORKING OUT THE MOVEMENT I sketched this horse on paper first, primarily to clarify my thoughts on how I planned to paint it. I practiced sketching many legs in movement because I was curious to see how they might look as a blur if I decided to paint them that way.

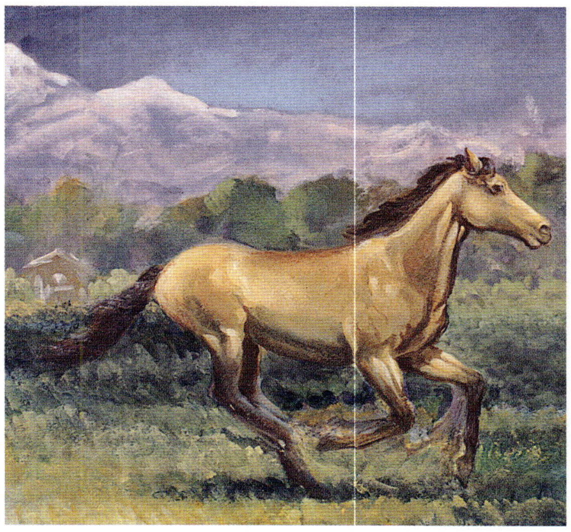

ADDING ACTION Here I used drybrush on the legs to accent their movement and added some drybrush to the flowing lines of the mane and tail. Then I introduced another "action" element: asymmetry. Because the horse is off-center, the horse seems to be galloping out of the scene!

Showing Action with Drybrush

Drybrush allows me to pick up the texture of the painting surface (especially if I'm using rough-textured watercolor paper), and it also makes it easy to create the blurred brushstrokes that impart a sense of movement, as I did on the painting of the galloping horse. I don't mean that you should blur all the forms so that it looks like a cartoon character with legs churning like a locomotive; just that you soften some of the edges and details so the moving subject looks just the way it would if you were viewing it in person—a little bit out of focus.

Painting Skies

SKIES CAN BE NEARLY ANY COLOR. In daytime, the colors you see will depend on the time of day and whether you are looking out toward the horizon or up above your head. And don't be fooled into thinking that the phrase "black of night" means "devoid of color"; some of the most compelling paintings focus on the luminous blues and greens of a nighttime sky. When I paint during the day, I find that the most interesting skyscapes are those that are filled with clouds, and acrylic is perfect for depicting their translucency.

Showcasing Daytime Clouds

Clouds will reflect some of the colors of the sky, so before I start painting clouds, I need to establish the sky colors. Looking toward the horizon, morning skies often have a yellowish, warm-neutral glow that becomes more turquoise and dull pink as midday approaches. Evening sky colors are similar to those of the morning, but the reds and pinks are more intense. Once I've laid in the sky colors, I'm ready to add the clouds, but I don't block them in as puffy circles of cotton. I always keep in mind that clouds have form, with a distinct top, side, and base, and I make them look more realistic by overlapping them to create a sense of depth.

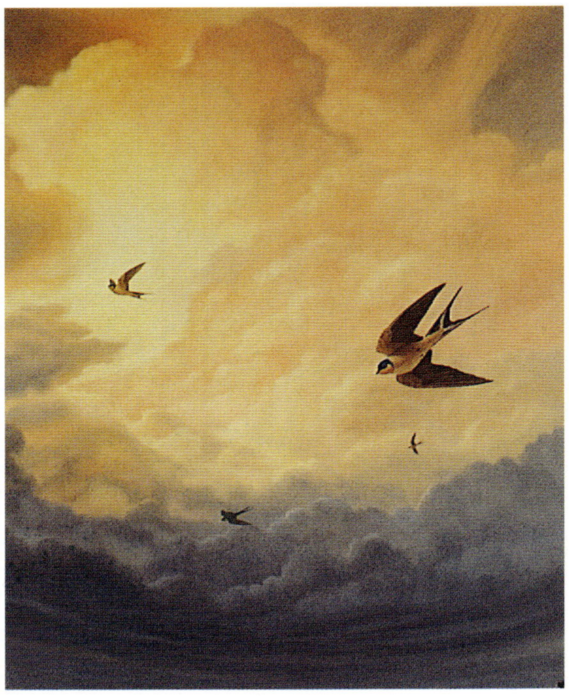

▲ **CREATING BRILLIANT WHITES** This thunderhead is an example of the way bright clouds in the distance can glow in yellows and reds. If you tried to achieve this effect without using at least some yellow or orange, the clouds would look too pasty-white and unrealistic.

▼ **STARTING WITH THE SKY** Using primed canvas paper, I painted in a daytime sky first, using deep cobalt blues at the top and blending into a pinkish turquoise at the horizon. For the mass of ground tone, I used a dark purple. I lightly drew in the clouds with a white pastel pencil, painting in the whole mass first. Then I added grays by mixing ultramarine blue, cadmium orange, and white right on the canvas. At the same time that I completed the landscape, I also refined the clouds by adding a little yellow and pink to the lightest areas so they wouldn't look pasty. To create soft transitions between the cloud bases, sides, and tops, I used my finger dipped in wet paint as a blending tool.

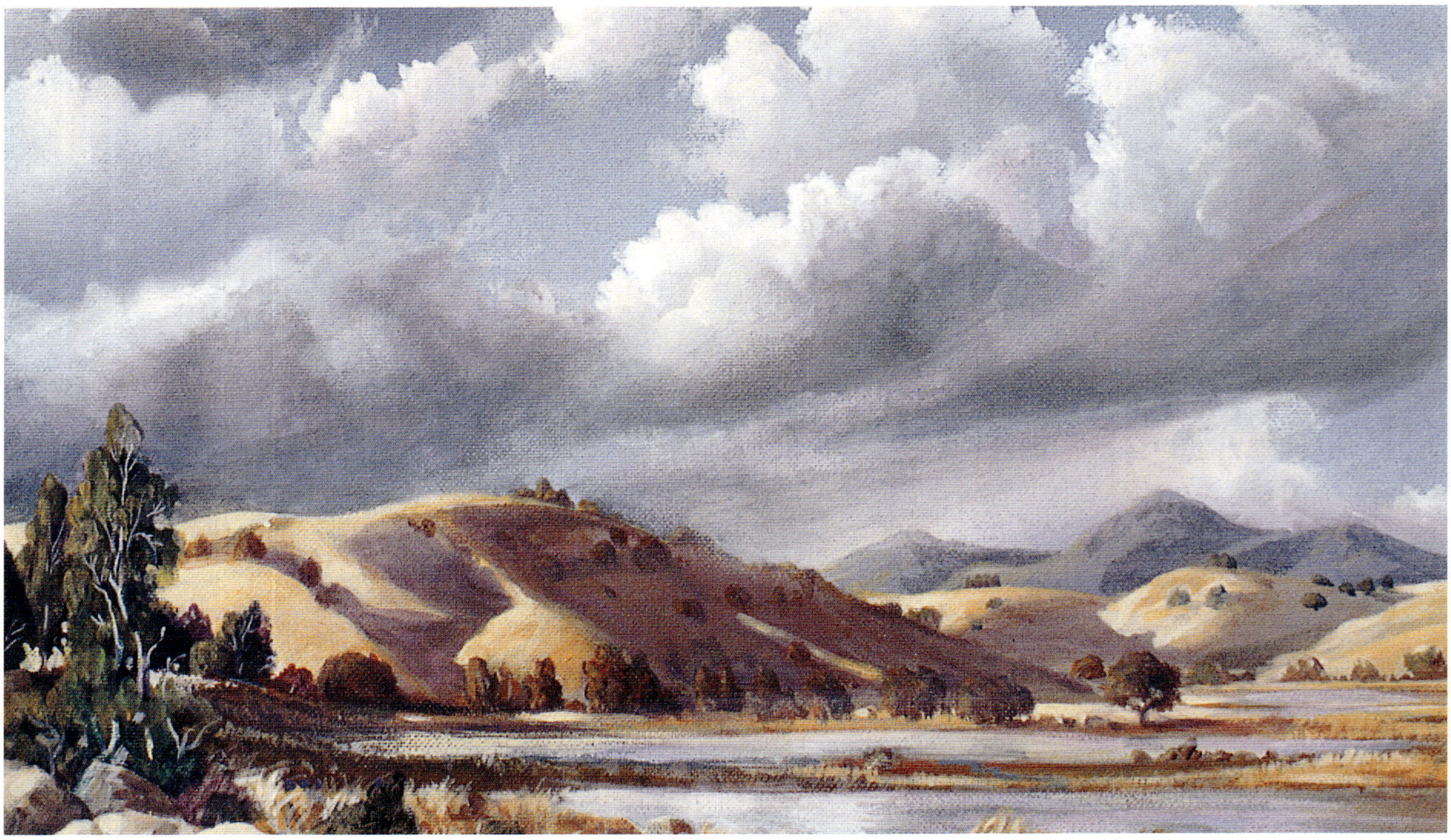

▸ **BUILDING A CLOUD** First paint a blue background; then drybrush cloud shapes over it using titanium white. Allow a little of the blue to show through.

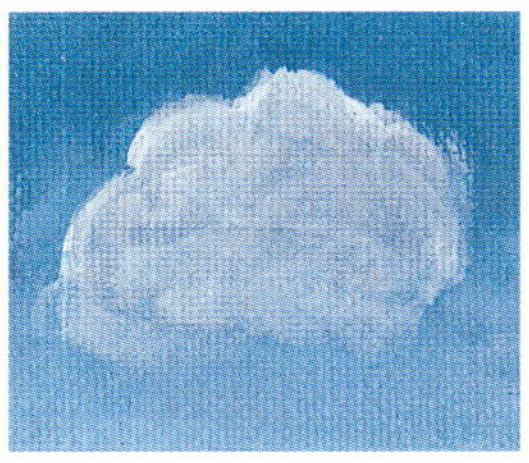

▸ **GIVE IT FORM** Next mix orange and ultramarine blue with white to make the gray of the cloud base. Use a little retarder to slow the drying time if necessary.

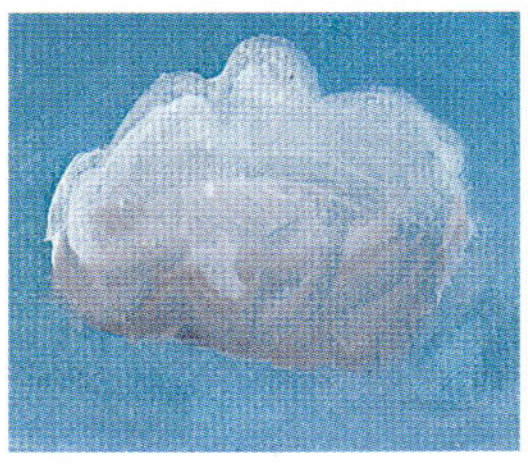

▸ **ADD BRILLIANCE** Add a touch of orange to the white so it looks more brilliant, and add a little pumice dust for drybrushing. Finish by adding accents as needed.

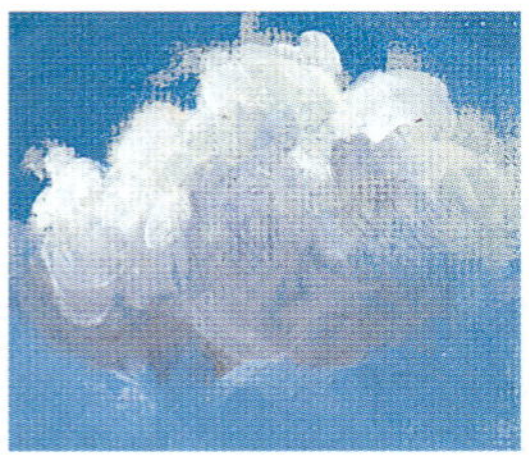

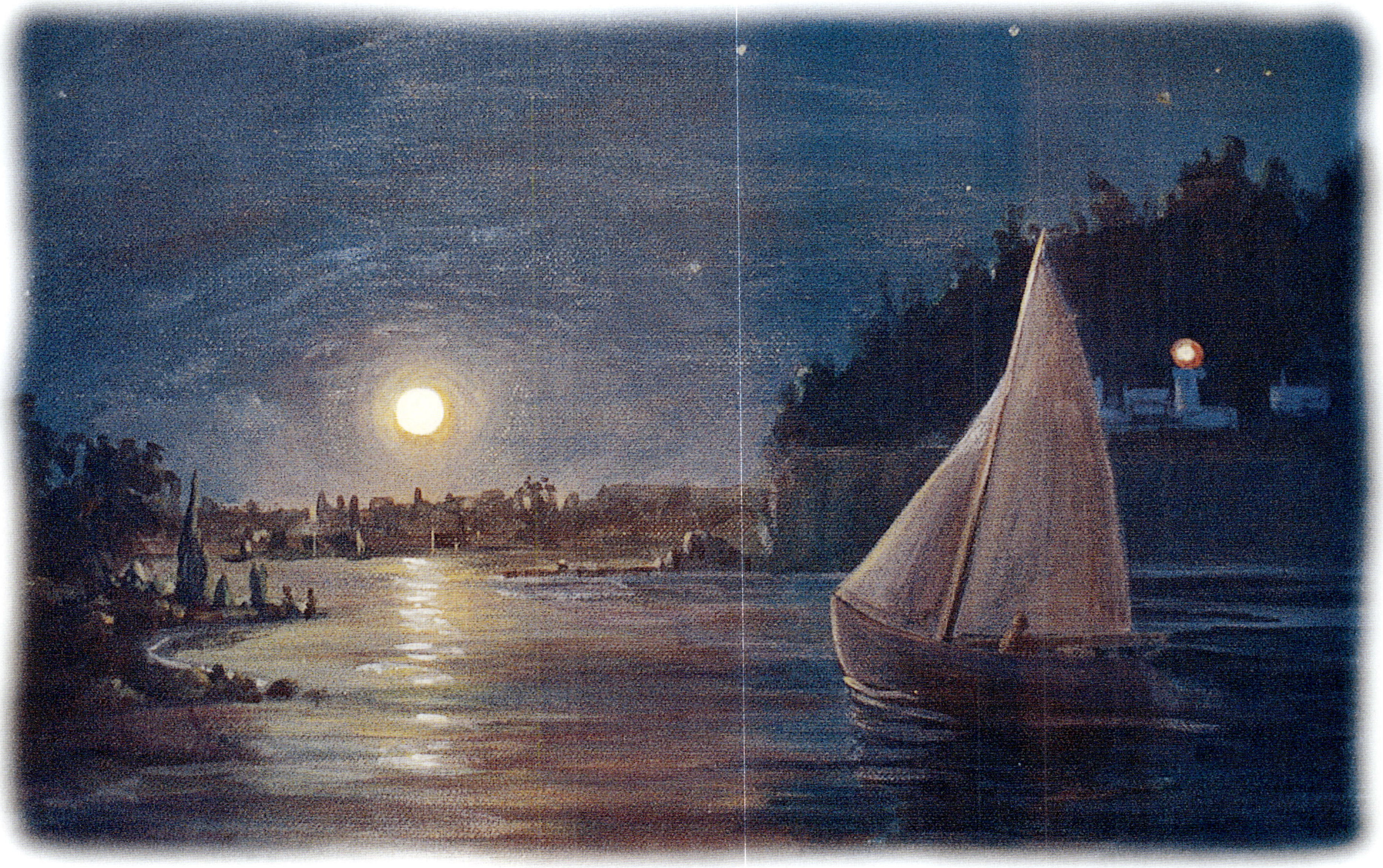

GLAZING As a final touch, I painted a light transparent wash, called a *glaze*, of burnt sienna over the foreground to show how moonlight adds a dull warmth.

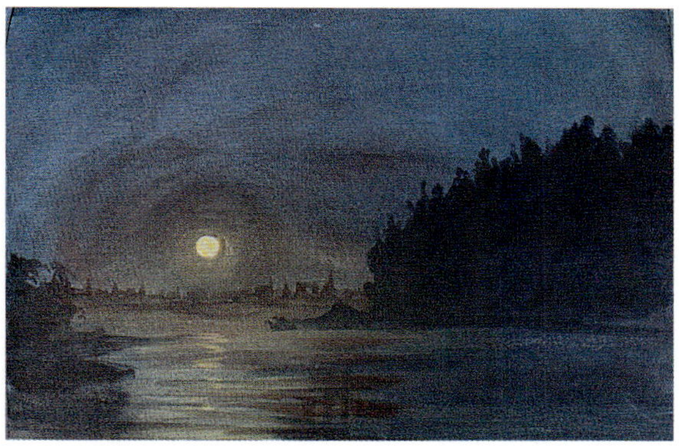

◀ **STARTING OUT** Using a flat brush and a night-sky palette (right), I toned a sheet of primed canvas paper, leaving a luminous warm area where I then put the moon. I painted the city and pine trees with a mixture of ultramarine, burnt sienna, and raw sienna.

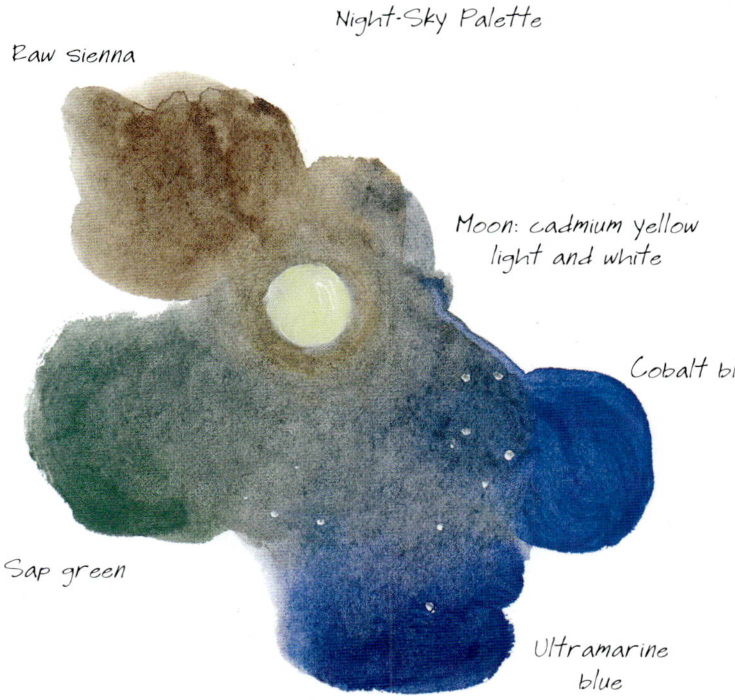

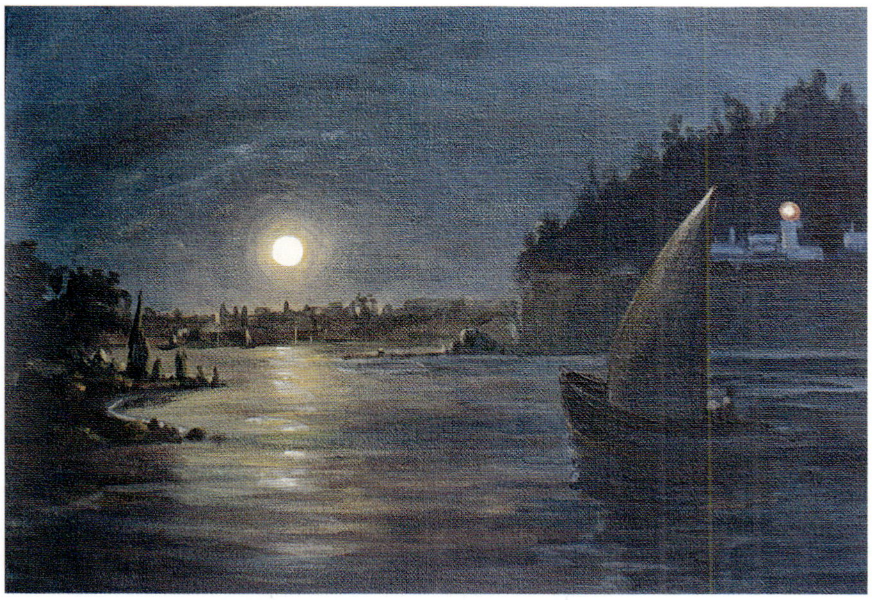

DEVELOPING THE SCENE With the sky painted in, I added an invented background, the moon, a sailboat, and a bank of pine trees. Next I painted in the cliff with raw umber and ultramarine blue. I mixed burnt sienna and white for the halo on the distant beacon, and used a mixture of white and burnt sienna to show moonlight on the distant city.

Depicting the Nighttime Sky

Night isn't black, and it isn't just dark blue either. If you really look from the horizon to the zenith (directly overhead), you will see that the night sky is a mixture of deep ultramarine blue, cobalt blue, sap green, and—when the moon is out—raw sienna. Just as it is during the day, the horizon's color is a little lighter and warmer than the zenith's, with an addition of raw or burnt sienna. I use the same group of colors for foliage, structures, or anything else in a nighttime scene. For the bright accents and the translucent moonlight, I add white and yellow to the mix.

Lighting Up Interiors

WHAT I LIKE MOST about painting interior scenes in acrylics is showing the different effects of light and cast shadows. I am fascinated by the different patterns that are revealed, making everyday objects—such as a chair or a handbag—seem attractive and more important. In fact, spots of light and shadows actually become an element of the composition, as they can add a lot of interest and texture. And speaking of texture, I often use both drybrush and painting knife techniques (see page 8) to add different textures to my interiors.

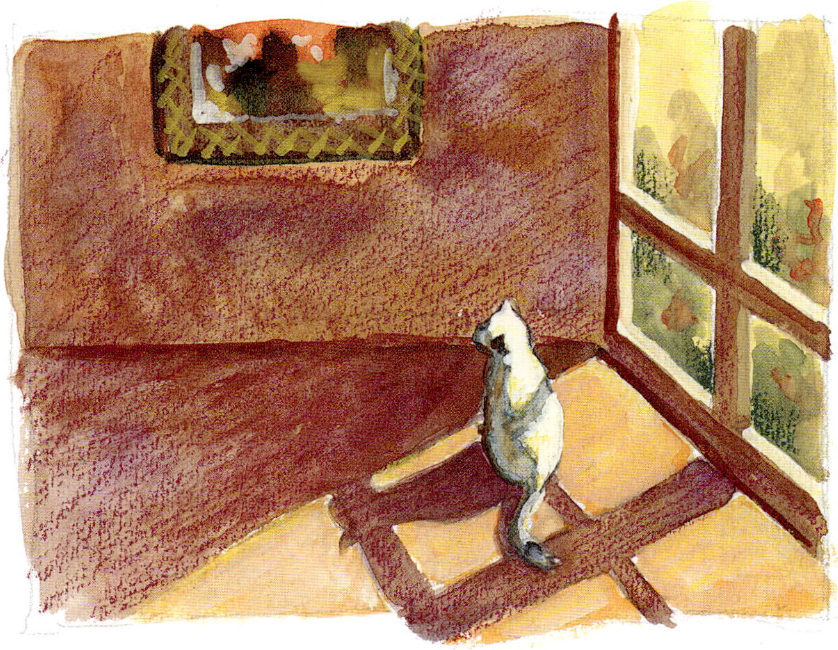

PAINTING SHADOW COLORS Shadows contain both the complementary opposite of the color of the light source and a bit of the color of the object they fall on. Here the shadows cast by the warm sunlight appear blue-gray on the white cat but become more purple (with brown overtones) on the ochre floor and wall (see color swatches below).

Utilizing a Single Light Source

I think light is one of the most important elements in a painting. Light not only helps define the forms of my subjects, it also sets the atmosphere, or mood, of the entire painting. I use a strong directional light source—whether natural or artificial—when I want high contrast and drama, because it creates very bright light areas and long, deep shadows. Notice how the contrast of the dark shadows in the paintings on these pages makes the highlights seem more brilliant.

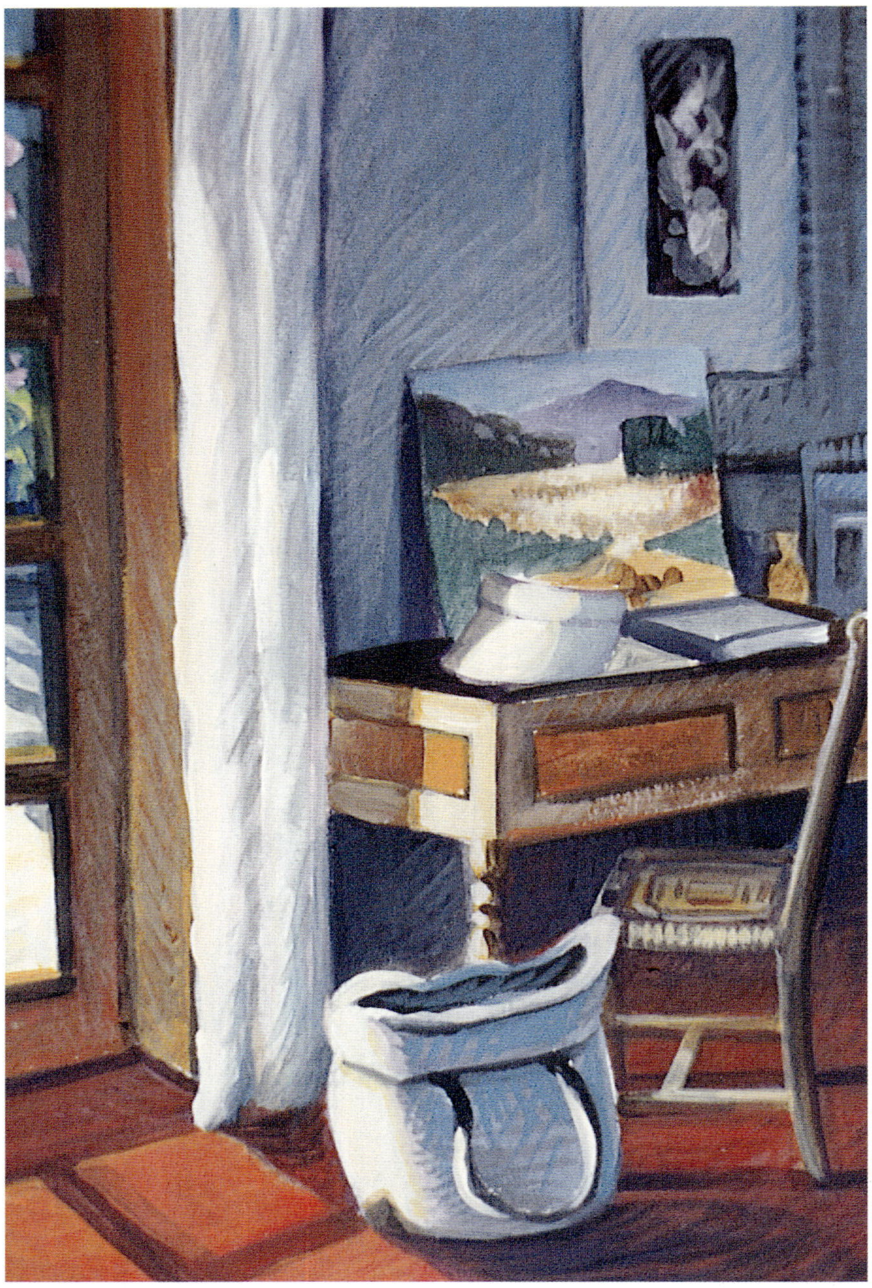

DRYBRUSHING After blocking in the shapes, I refined the forms using crosshatching and a very dry brush. To re-create the lighting, I used lighter strokes over dark areas and darker strokes over light areas.

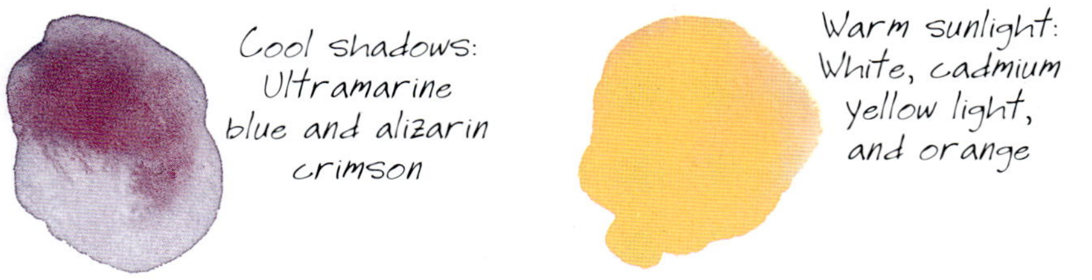

Painting Cast Shadows

Cast shadows are easy to paint once you know how they work. Shadows aren't single-toned areas of even color; they weaken in strength as they leave their source, so they vary in color and intensity. For example, in the detail study for the painting of my studio at right, notice that the edges of the maroon shadow start out hard and dark but get increasingly lighter and softer. This is because ambient light (light from surrounding areas) bounces back into the shadows on the floor and bag and lightens them most where they are weakest.

▼ **APPLYING SHADOW COLORS** Since a cast shadow is very dark, I painted this one on top of the red I had blocked in for the floor. I used burnt umber and alizarin crimson to darken the shadow color, making the area closest to the bag the darkest. I also kept the edges hard at first and softened them more the farther they got from the bag.

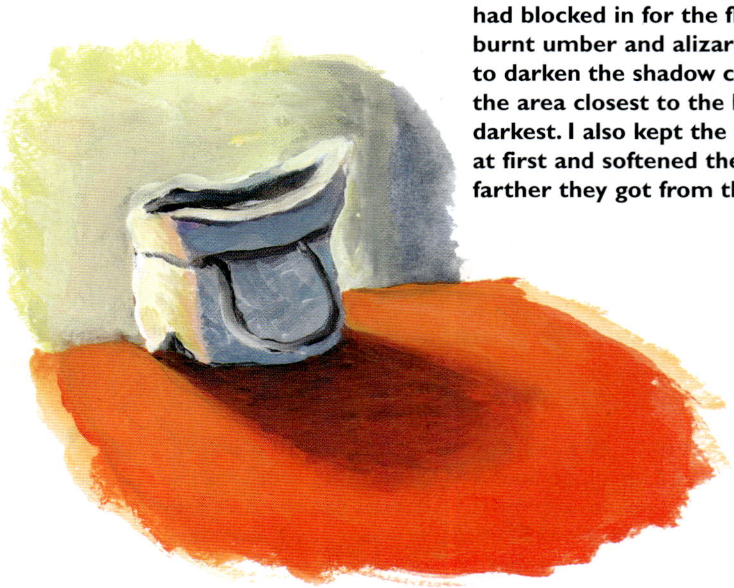

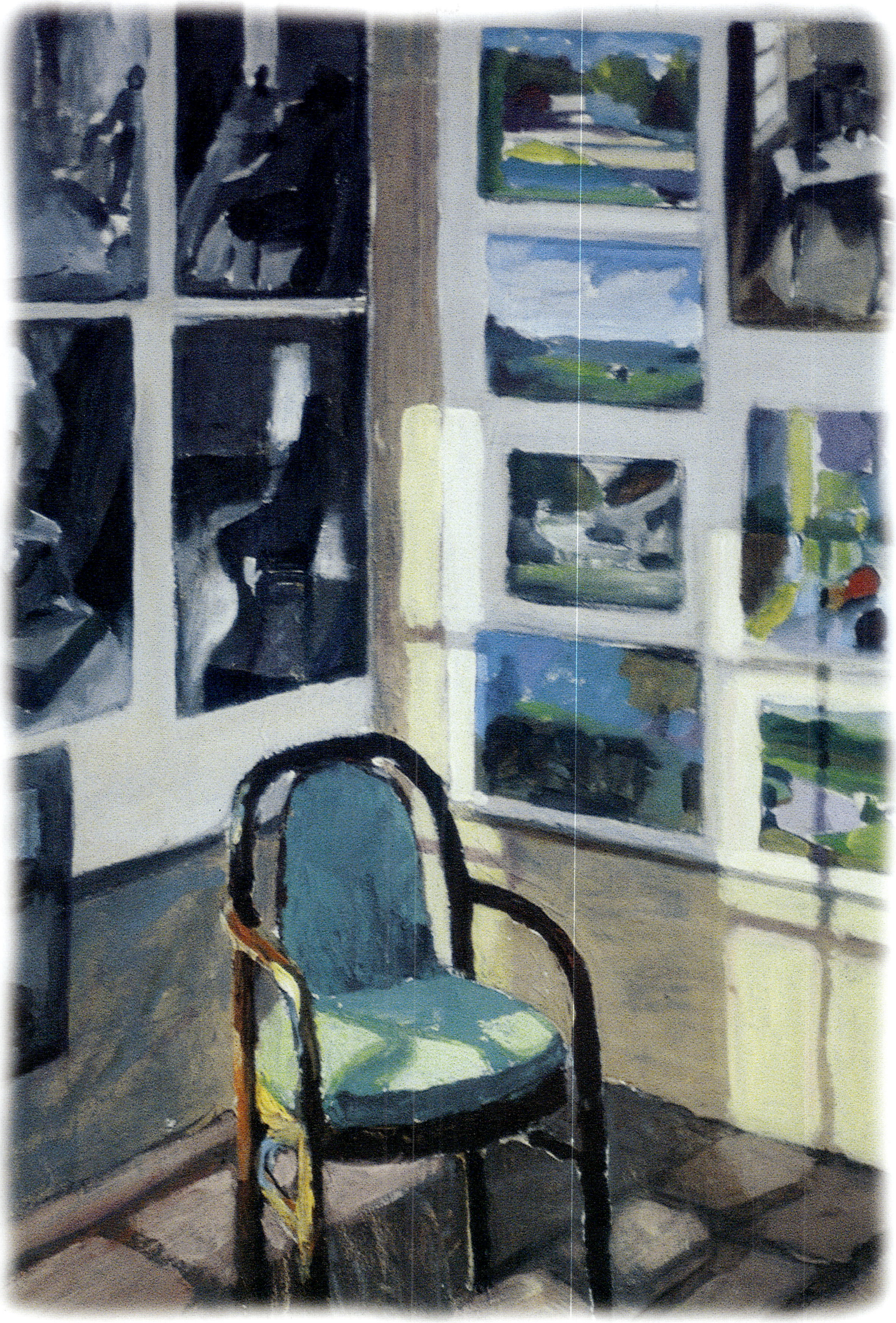

CAPTURING THE CHANGING LIGHT
Keep in mind that natural light changes rapidly so you'll need to work quickly. I was attracted to these morning shadows, but by the time I set up my paints, all that was left was their memory. I had to paint everything I could see then, and I waited for the next morning to capture the light and shadow patterns.

Focusing on Structures

BUILDINGS CAN BE just as stimulating to paint as forms found in nature. In fact, I really think a successful painting hinges more on composition and lighting than it does on a particular type of subject. For example, paintings like the ones shown here do not depict extraordinary pieces of architecture, but they do demonstrate how somewhat ordinary buildings painted from various viewpoints can still have unique compositions, vivid patterns of light and shadow, and interesting design qualities all their own.

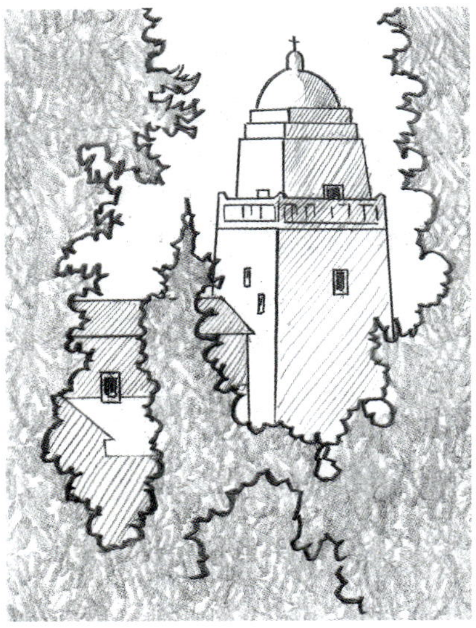

OVERLAPPING I used sketches to work out the natural framing created by the pines. They give a feeling of being there—an intimate view of the scene.

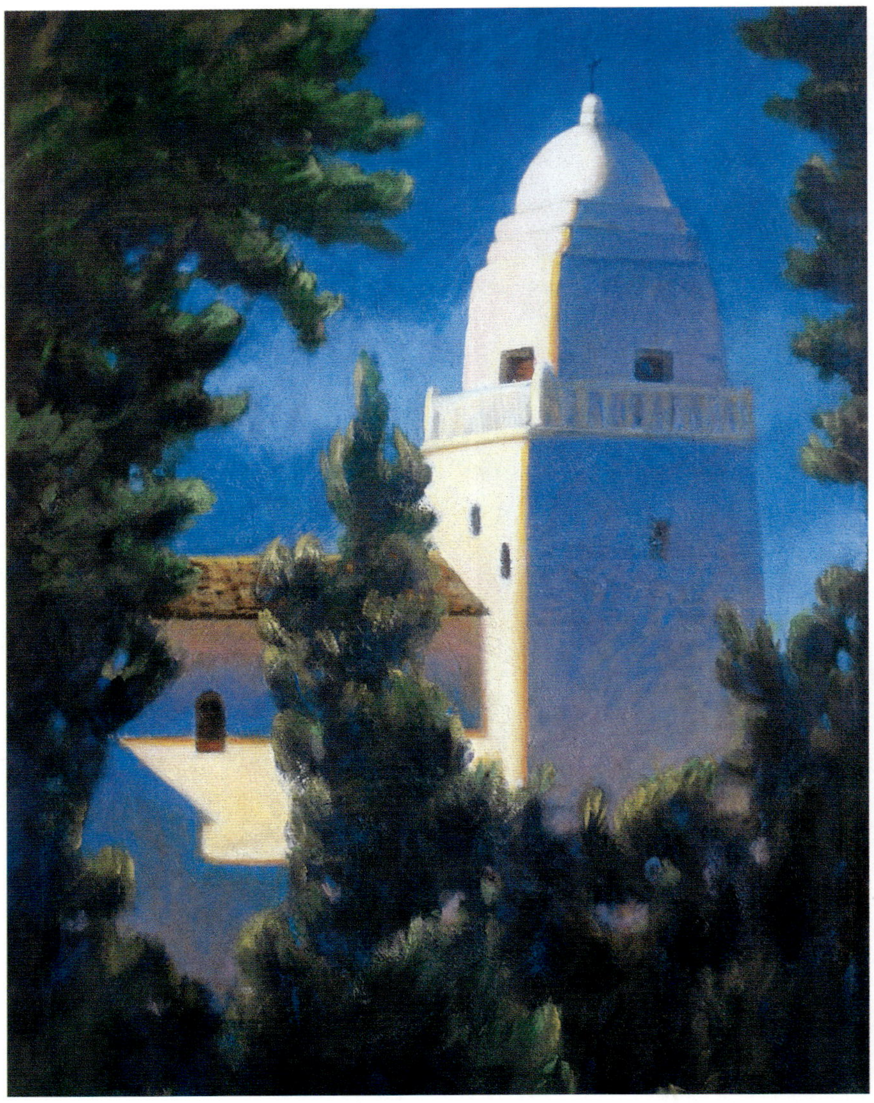

TAKING A CLOSEUP VIEW When working up close, your subject will be large and the perspective more subtle. With this viewpoint, I had a chance to focus on the textures, and I used dramatic lighting to accentuate the architectural lines of the structure.

Showing Dimension in Buildings

I have three main methods of creating a sense of depth in my paintings, which I use either singly or, more often, in combination. I use *linear perspective* to lead the viewer's eye into the distance (see the box on one-point perspective). I overlap objects, which makes objects in front come forward and objects behind recede, creating a feeling of space. And I apply *atmospheric perspective* (the fact that distance tends to obscure details and make things look bluer) to make background elements recede. One of the great things about acrylic is that you can use thicker paint for objects in the foreground, and you can use thin transparent glazes to show the effects of atmosphere in the distance.

► **USING ATMOSPHERIC PERSPECTIVE** Here I used both color and detail to enhance the sense of depth. Note how the warm greens make the grass come forward, while the cool purples cause the skyline to recede. I also added details to the foliage in front and made the distant buildings soft and hazy.

Ultramarine blue with a little alizarin crimson and white

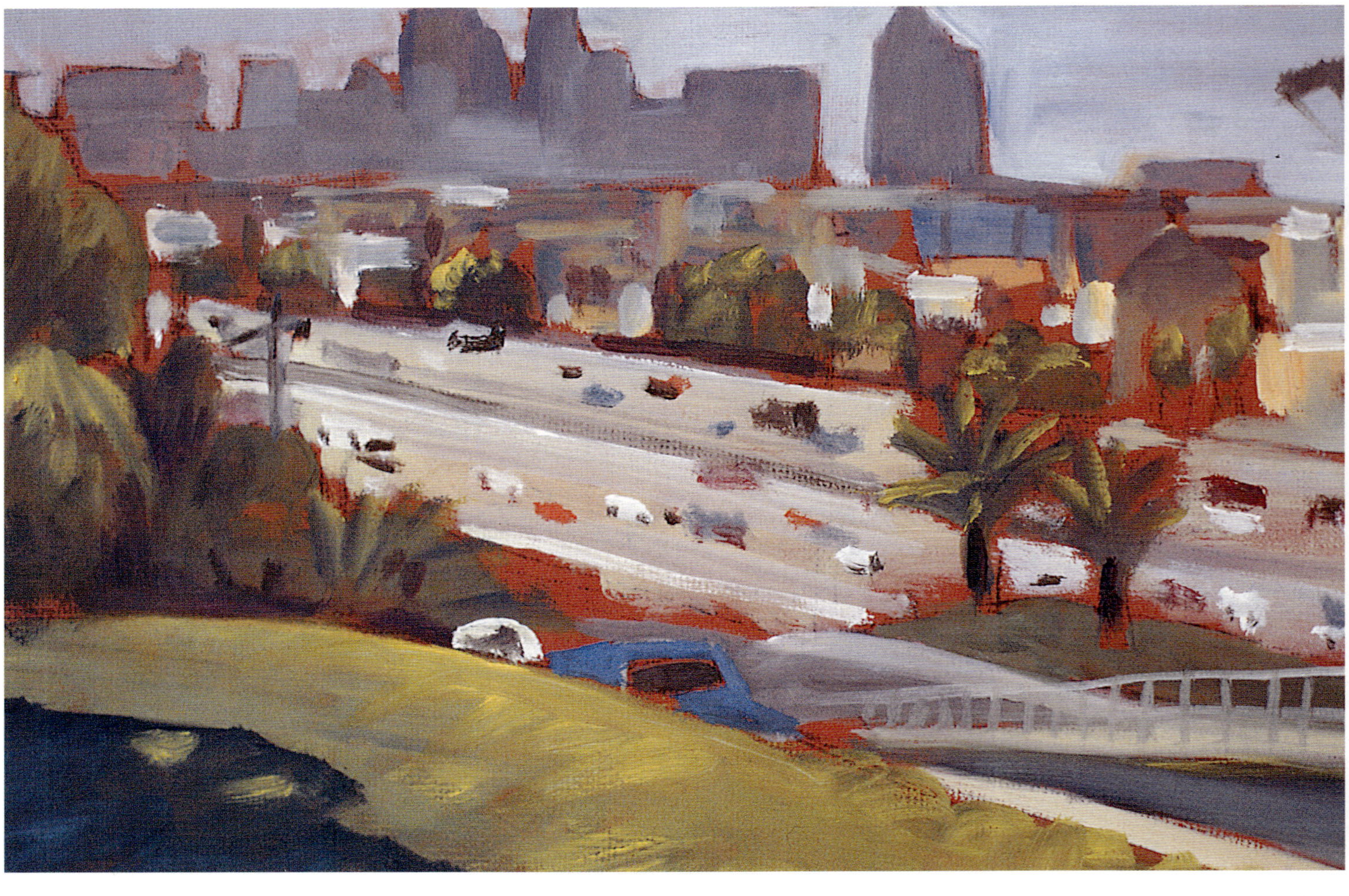

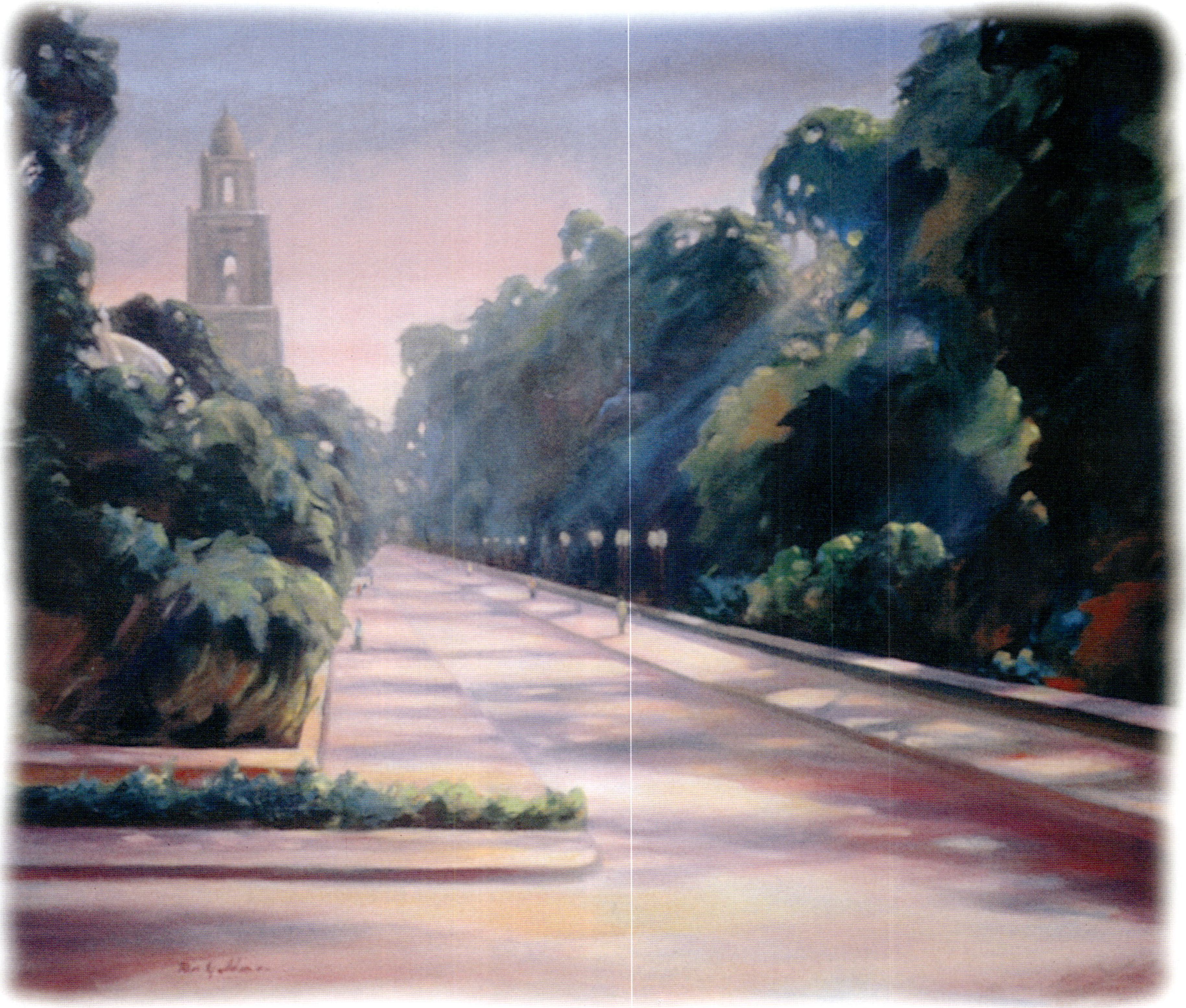

One-Point Perspective

Perspective refers to creating the illusion of three dimensions on a two-dimensional surface, and the most fundamental and simplest form of perspective is called *one-point perspective.* The "one point" means you pick one point on the horizon, called the *vanishing point* (VP), and make all the parallel lines in your painting recede to that point. Here's how to do it. Draw a horizontal line across your picture to represent eye level (this is your horizon line). Place a point on the horizon line (for instance, put it in the middle third of your picture's width, as shown at right) to represent the vanishing point—the point all your parallel lines will "vanish," or recede, to. Now draw light lines from your subject to the vanishing point, as shown here. Fit your drawing to these lines and you've created a sense of dimension.

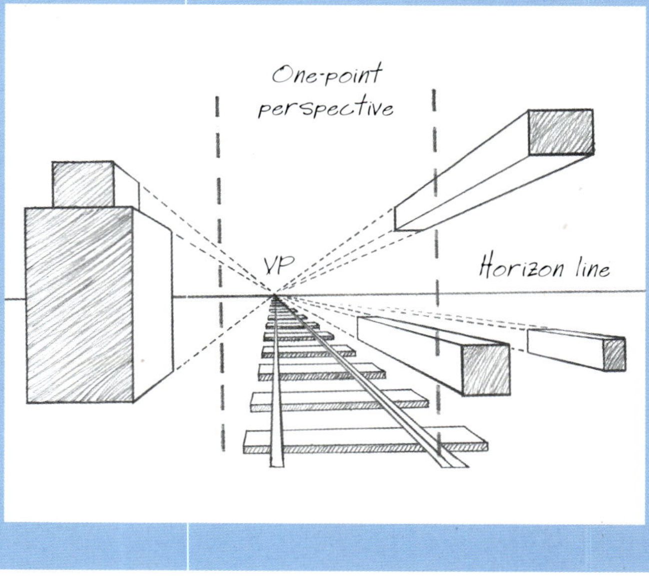

▲ COMBINING METHODS **In this painting, I used all three methods of creating depth. The road is an example of linear perspective, the blurred trees and tower demonstrate atmospheric perspective, and the arrangement of the elements shows overlapping at work. The distant light rays were glazed in with transparent blue, green, and violet.**

Making Lively Still Lifes

STILL LIFES OFFER A GREAT opportunity to learn and practice new painting skills. I can experiment with new strokes, test out a variety of color combinations, apply interesting textures, and practice setting up dynamic compositions. I can work whenever I want without concern about the light changing, and I don't have to worry about my subject staying still. And, because acrylic dries so quickly, I don't have to wonder whether my flower subjects will wilt while I wait for a section to dry—I can finish an entire painting in one session!

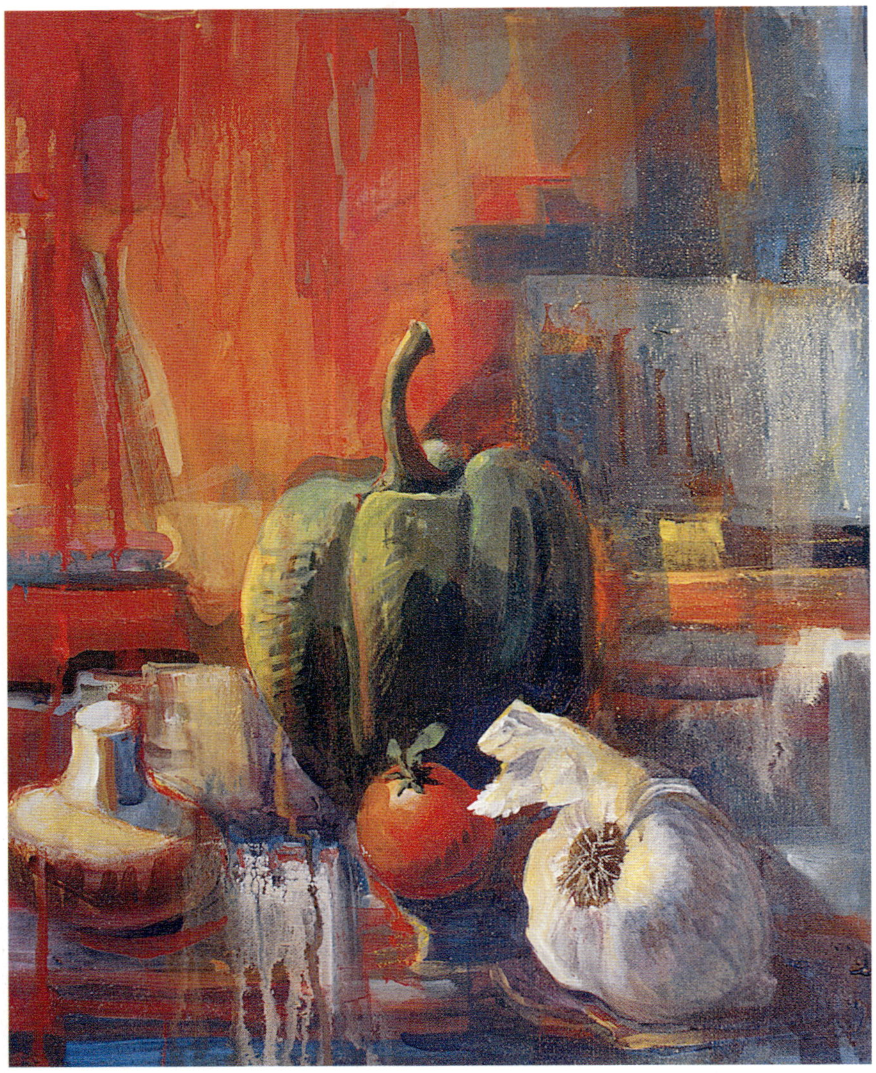

PAINTING WITH WASHES This painting went through a number of changes, and part of its richness is due to the remnants of a blue background under the warm colors on top. Most of this painting was done with thin, drippy washes of very diluted paint, but I added texture with brushstrokes of thicker paint in the upper right, and I made patterns on the bottom by scraping with a palette knife for variation.

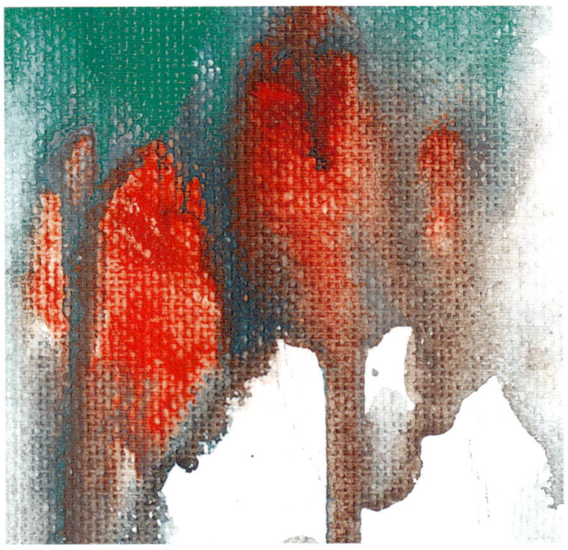

► **EMBRACING ACCIDENTS** Here is an example of the kind of happy accident that occured in the painting above, which added interest and texture. To encourage these accidents, I render the forms realistically at first, then deliberately lose some of the hard edges with washes. I made the drips shown here by squishing a brush loaded with wet paint into a wet area and seeing what happened.

Taking Advantage of Negative Space

Have you ever had a drawing exercise where you drew everything around an object, rather than drawing the object itself? That is called *drawing the negative space*, as shown in the example below. Actually, I think these should be called "definitive spaces" because they not only define a form, they also set off a more active area of a painting by serving as a passive contrast. Just as in music there would be no composition without silence between the notes, still lifes (and other paintings as well) need calm areas to set off the active focal points. Sometimes when faced with a complicated still life to paint, the basic shapes are hidden by all the different patterns and textures. Drawing the negative spaces first allows me to find the outlines that seem to be hidden in so much visual information—it's another way to think and see things "outside the box."

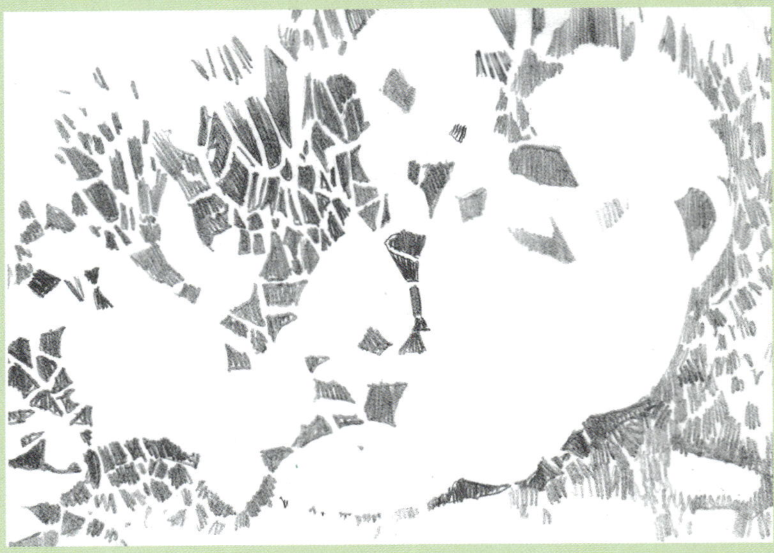

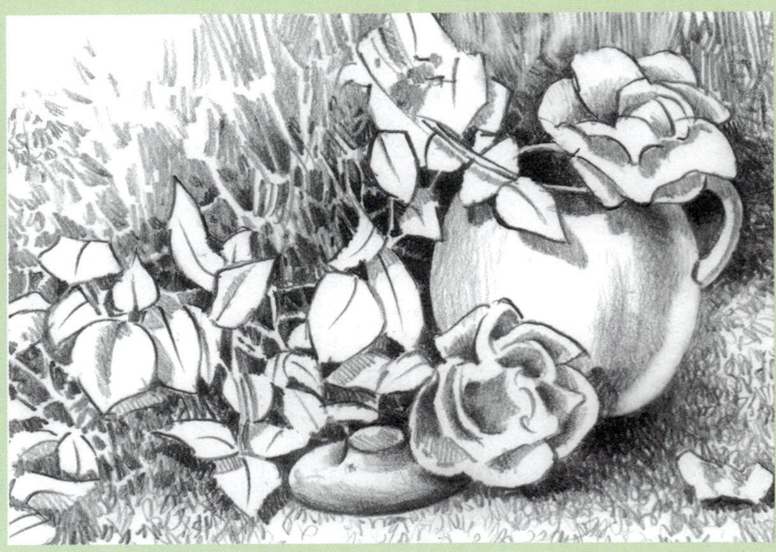

Letting the Paint Create Texture

I like the fast drying time of acrylic for my still lifes because I can change my mind and quickly paint over an area without being concerned about wet paint mixing into my new color. An added advantage is that the underlying paint creates extra texture that I wouldn't have had otherwise. But what I especially like about acrylic is the accidental textures I get when I let the paint drip and clot on its own. I used this to my advantage in the still life at upper left, where many of my favorite touches were accidents! Also try out impasto, scumbling, and other texturizing methods on page 8 to create interesting backgrounds that will enhance your still lifes.

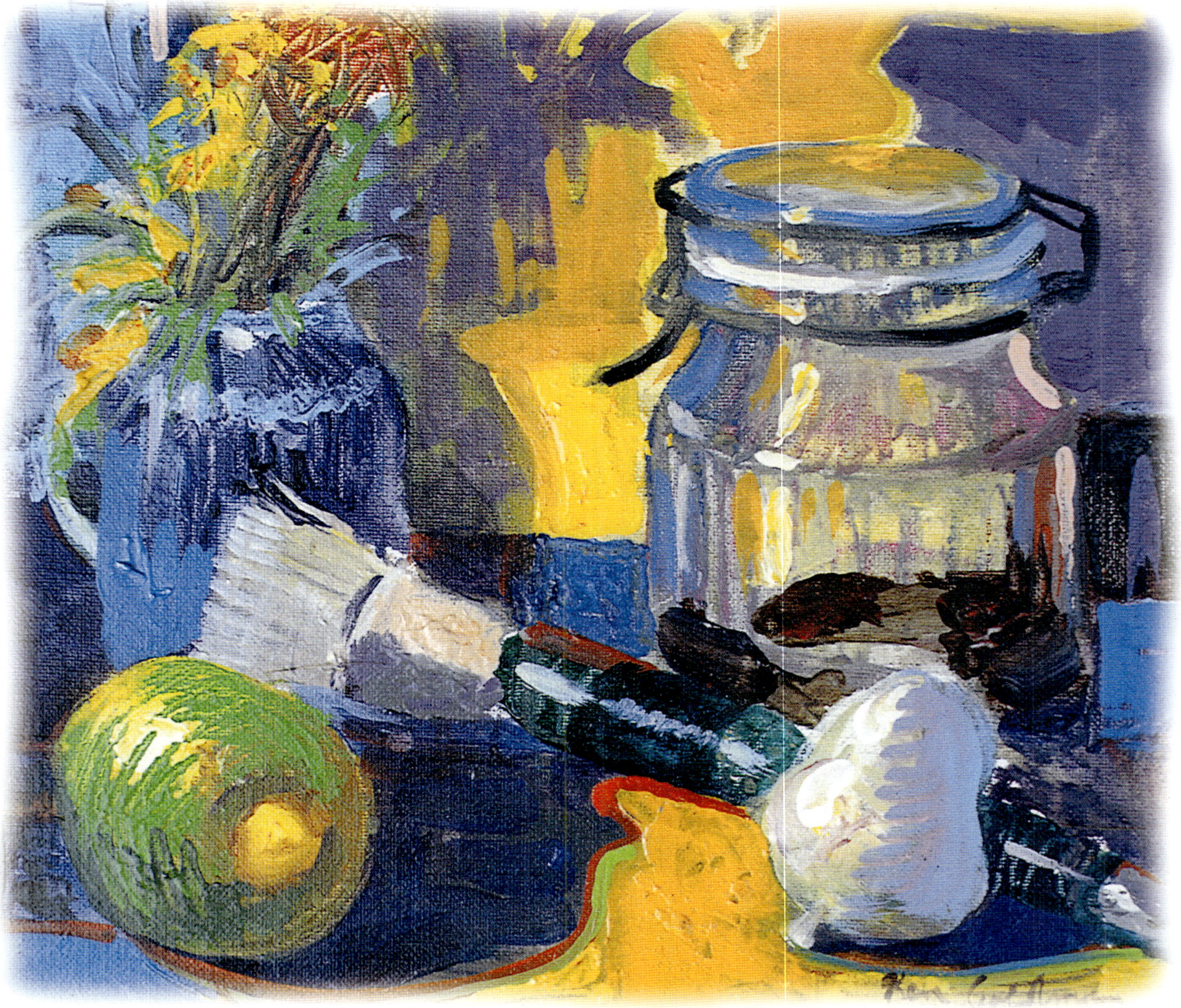

◄ USING A KNIFE I finished this painting with a palette knife. For the flowers in the brown pot on the left, I used the knife to scrape away paint and to add texture. For everything else, I used the knife to pile on thick color.

Artist's Tip

Sometimes the best still lifes are "found." Paint whatever happens to be on the table, mantel, kitchen counter, or window sill for a spontaneous grouping.

▼ CREATING CONTRASTS This little painting works because it has just about every contrast imaginable: in color, texture, form, angles, and value.

Setting Up a Simple Still Life

You don't have to contrive complicated setups to make an interesting still life. There is just as much beauty and life in a simple grouping of objects, such as the peppers to the right, which I helped make lively by using three peppers instead of four (there is more excitement in an odd-numbered grouping than an even one). What makes a still life "lively" is largely a matter of creating some visual excitement by using (either singly or in combination): asymmetrical composition, diagonal lines, varying shapes and sizes, dynamic lighting, complementary colors, and interesting brushstrokes. When you look at the two drawings below, you will see how asymmetry is used to create interest.

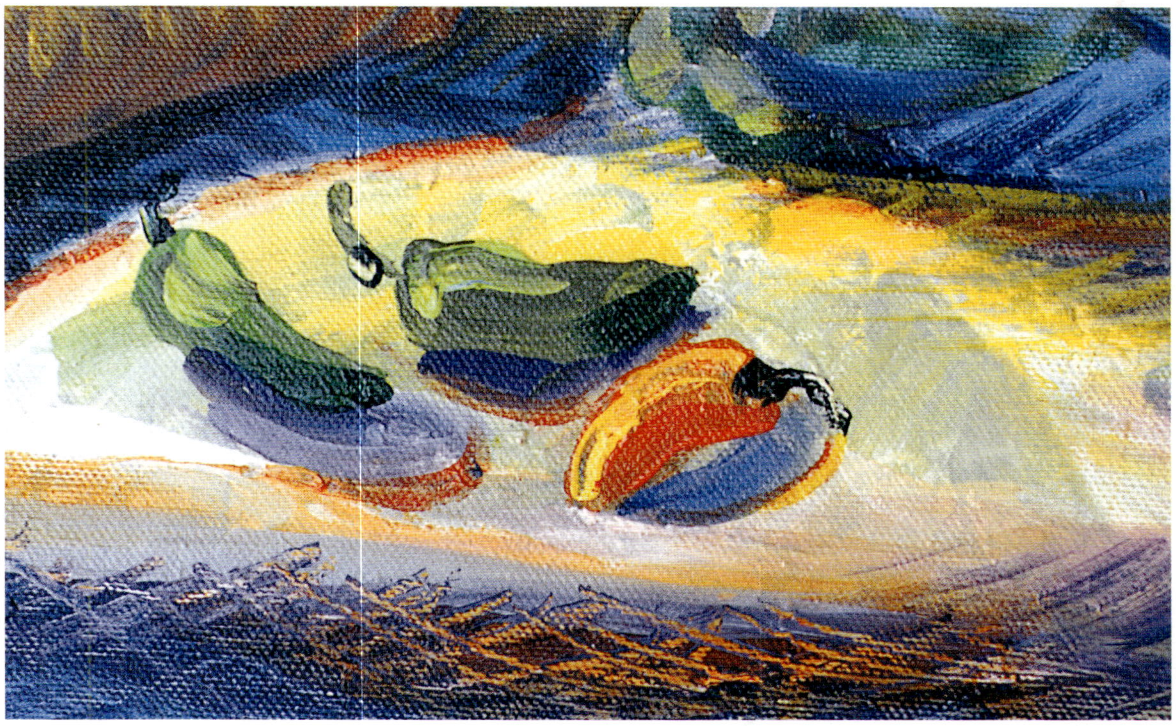

► WORKING WITH ASYMMETRY This thumbnail shows how basic forms placed unevenly create interest and movement. In our culture, we read from left to right, so the eye looks first to the fruit on the left, then to the vase, and on to the mug.

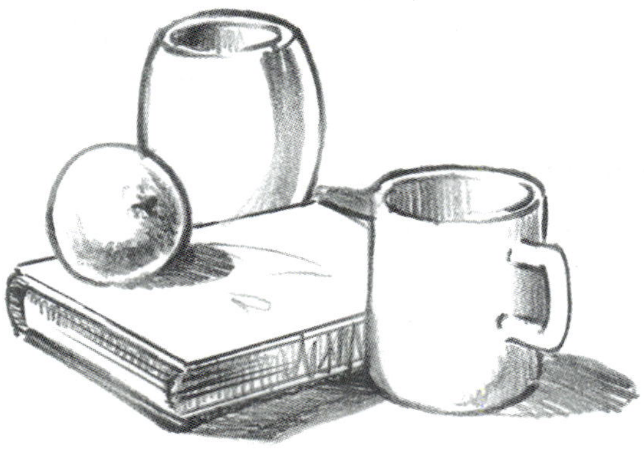

► USING TOO MUCH SYMMETRY When all the same objects are too evenly spaced, the eye does not circulate. The eye goes from left to right and then straight out of the picture frame! Too much symmetry does not encourage the viewer to linger.

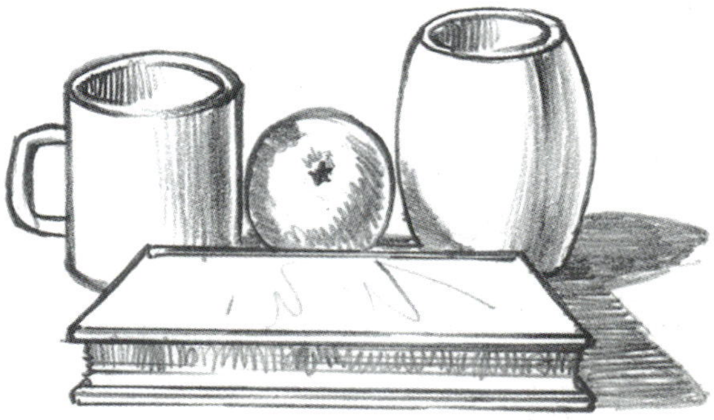

Introducing Portraiture

WHETHER PAINTING A FRIEND or a complete stranger, creating a portrait is no different than painting a still life, landscape, or animal. It's all a matter of learning how to mix and apply the colors and to paint what you *see*. Don't be too concerned if you don't get a perfect likeness all the time. A portrait that captures a likeness at the expense of expressiveness is not as successful as a portrait with great expressiveness and no likeness at all. The best way to master portraiture—or any other subject—is to practice a lot, and then practice some more. And have fun doing it!

Learning to Look

Success in painting means learning to paint what you really see, instead of painting the way you *think* your subject should look. Before you try painting a full portrait, start by turning a simple photo upside down and copying only the eyes, nose, and mouth area. This will free you from your preconceptions about what features should look like. When you turn your drawing right side up, you will be amazed at the resemblance that small area has captured. Learn to stare at your subject until you really see the shapes, and then apply your paint only when you are certain the shapes will mean something.

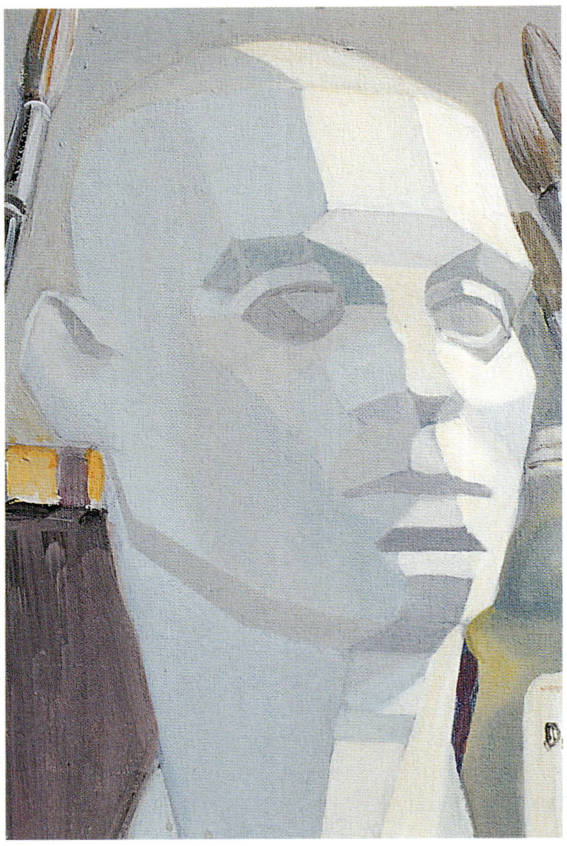

◄ STUDYING LIGHTING This plaster head (which is part of the painting on page 15) shows how the planes of the head look when they are illuminated from a single light source (coming from above right). Here you can see the way various facial planes catch direct light or show reflected light. This helps you determine where to place light, middle, and dark values for the skin.

▼ MIXING SKIN TONES People's skin tones are as varied as their features. The chart below shows a range of typical skin tones, from dark to light, and the colors I use to create them.

Alizarin crimson, raw umber, and sap green

Alizarin crimson and raw sienna

Alizarin crimson, sap green, and raw sienna

Alizarin crimson, sap green, raw sienna, and a little white

Raw sienna, cadmium red light, sap green, and a little white

Cadmium yellow light, cadmium red light, some white, and a little sap green

Cadmium yellow light, cadmium red light, and some white

White, cadmium yellow light, and cadmium red light

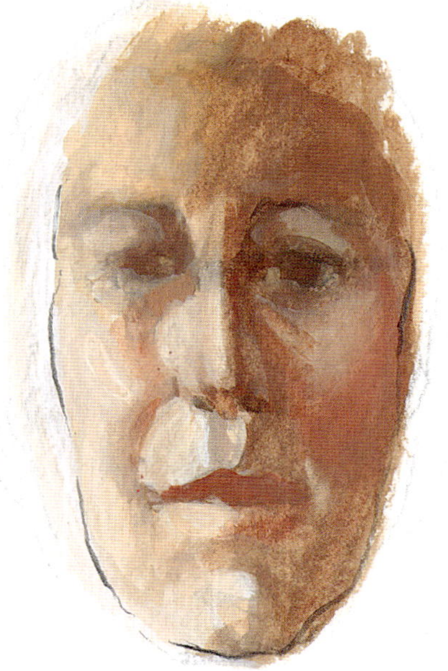

FACE Here the details are blurred and indistinct—just as they would look if you were viewing a face with your eyes squinted. Large, simple shapes come first; details come later.

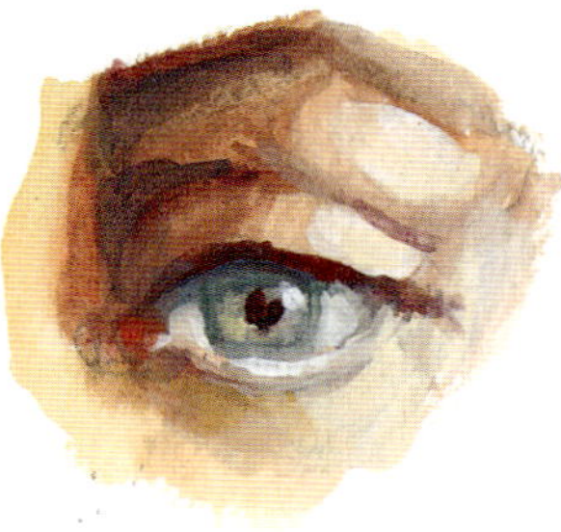

◄ EYES The eyeball is spherical, and the lids open and close over it. If there is a highlight on one side of the iris, there will be a small light area on the other side, as this example illustrates.

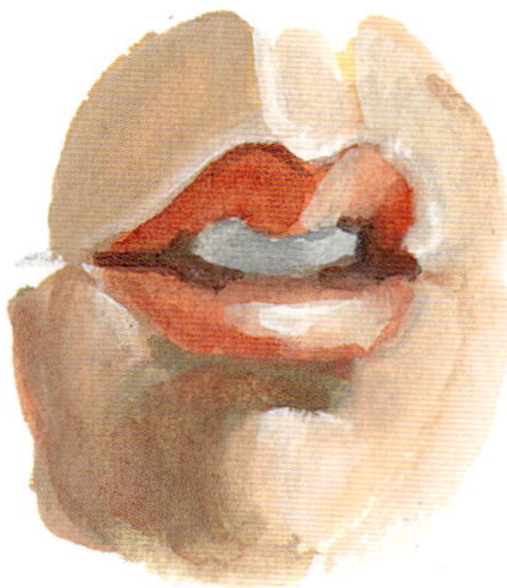

◄ MOUTH The lips sit on top of the curved form of the teeth. The profile shape is based on a person's overbite or underbite, so the upper lip usually protrudes more than the lower lip.

► NOSE When you paint a nose, first sketch it as a triangular wedge, the dominant shape of most noses. The nostrils are not as visible as you might think, so don't overemphasize them or you will have painted a snout instead of a nose!

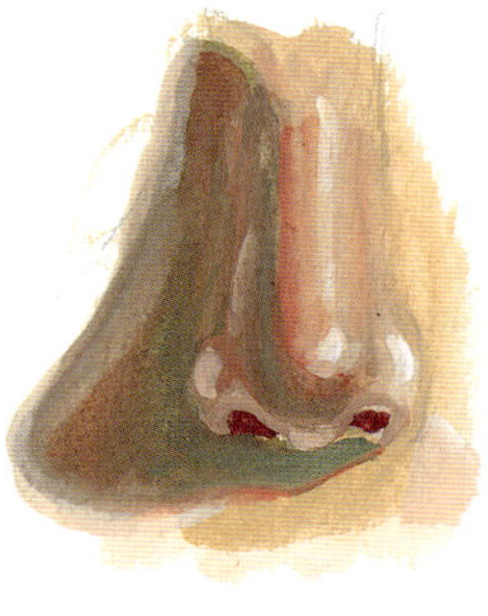

► EARS The ears slant back slightly and are divided into three parts: upper, middle, and lobe. The lobe can be quite red and fleshy, and the shape varies from individual to individual. Some lobes are attached to the head and some hang freely.

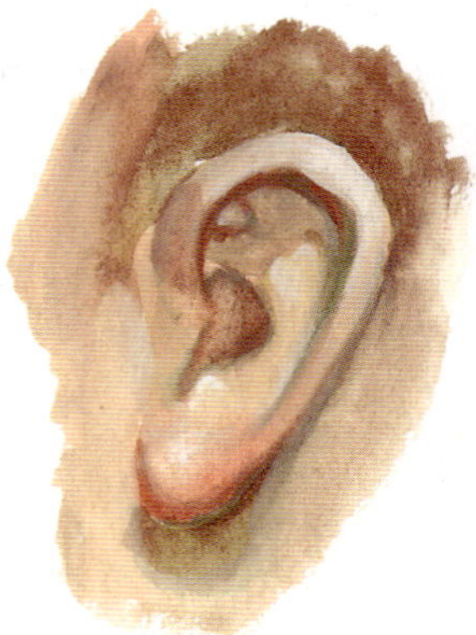

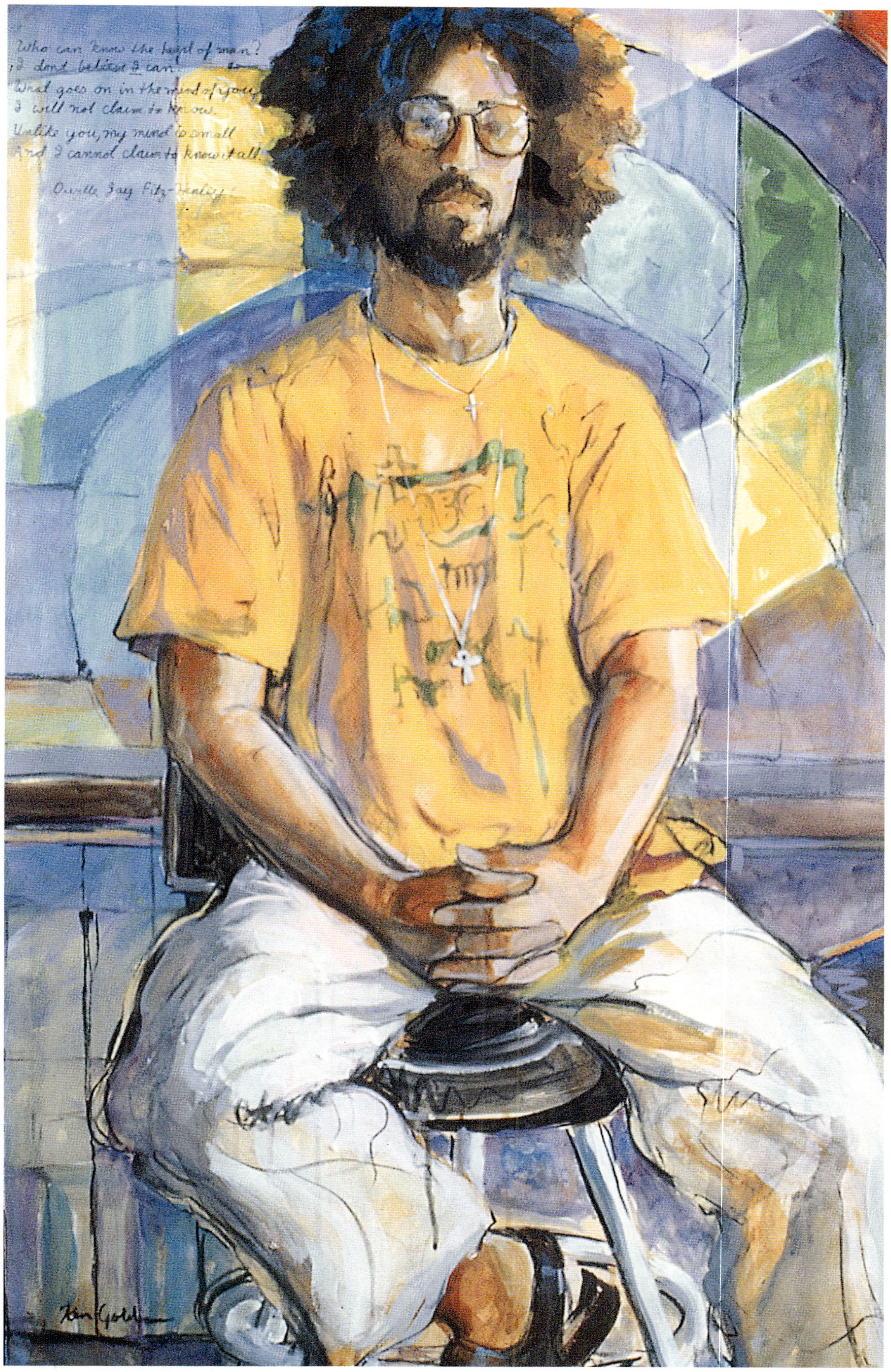

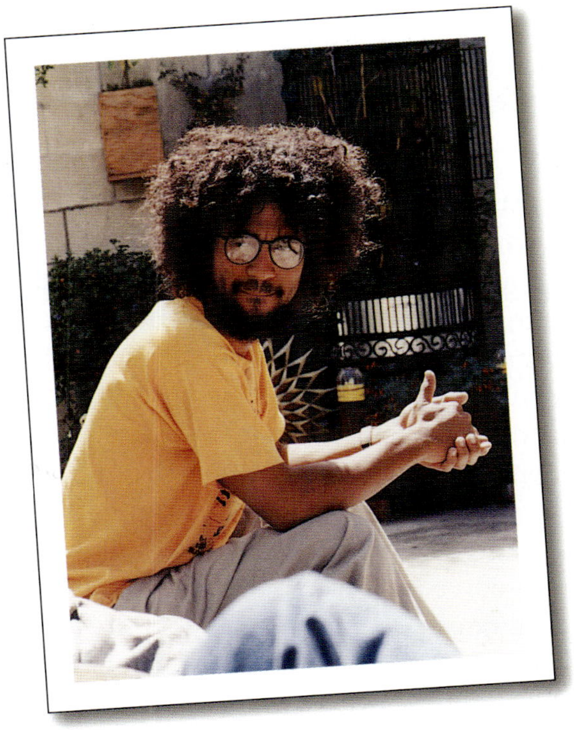

ARTISTIC LICENSE I wanted to paint a portrait of my friend, but I wasn't wild about the composition of this photo. Instead, I painted him facing forward so I could see him better, and used fairly strong lighting to illuminate his features.

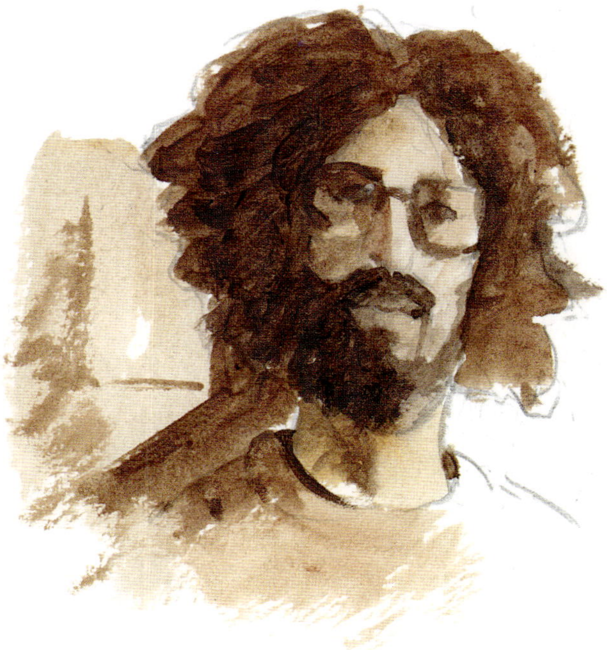

UNDERPAINTING I began this portrait by underpainting my subject with values of raw umber and white. This served two purposes: It primed and sealed the surface to make it less absorbent, so my top colors would be more vibrant, and it got me started on the painting.

FINISHING THE PORTRAIT Once the values were built up, I began to paint the flesh tones, starting with the lights and adding touches of blue and orange in the hair. Then I added the background design (derived from one of my paintings) to really make my subject stand out.

Lining Up to a Grid

Following a grid similar to the one shown at right can help you correctly place all the features in your portraits. In developing a likeness, you must constantly check vertical and horizontal alignment. For example, here a vertical plumb line shows that the corner of the mouth falls right below the center of the eye, and a horizontal line shows that the base of the ears (under the hair!) lines up with the bottom of the nose.

► **USING GUIDELINES** Proportional accuracy is only part of what makes a good painting—but it sure helps! Divide the oval of the head into thirds and use guidelines to help you place the features of the individual you are painting.

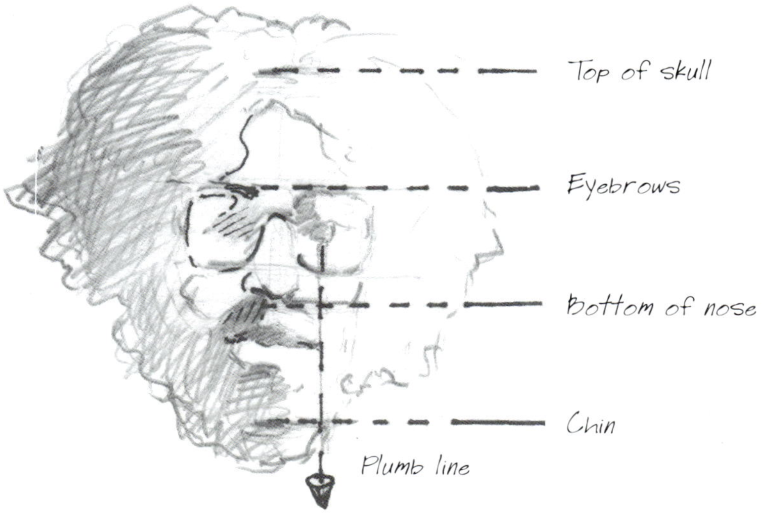

Creating a Self-Portrait

I AM THE MOST DEPENDABLE MODEL I know, which is one of the main reasons I like to paint self-portraits. Whenever the light is right, I can just go into my studio and work. People often say that I look mad or sad in my self-portraits, but nothing could be further from the truth. The look they see is concentration. People are used to my social side, good-natured and full of smiles; but it takes real concentration to be objective, and I paint what I see—like it or not!

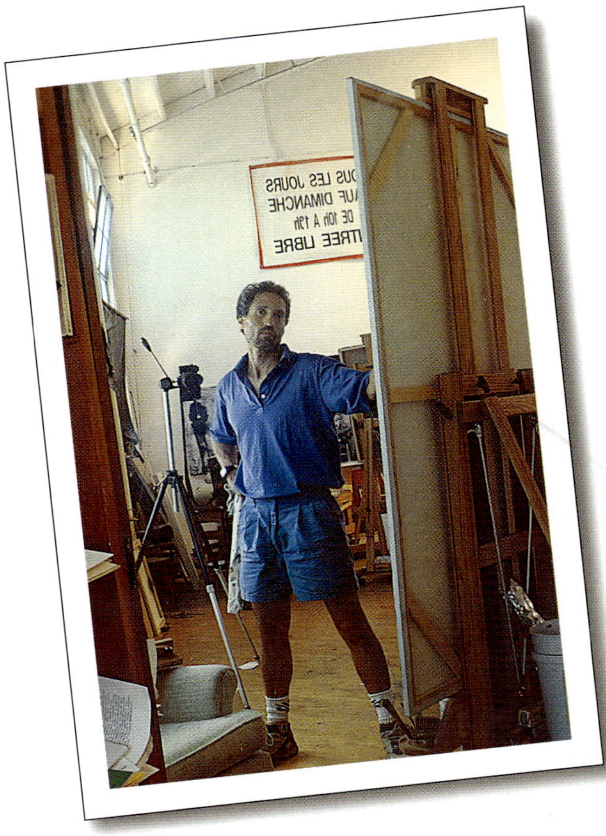

◄ **USING PHOTOS After I finished the self-portrait on page 31, I thought it might be a good idea to take a photograph for future reference. Notice that for the painting I changed the color of my shirt to better complement the color of my bird, perched on my shoulder.**

Seeing Yourself

We don't really see ourselves as others see us. We have to look in a mirror, and mirrors reflect things in reverse, which is why I appear to be left-handed in my self-portraits! If this is your first time painting a self-portrait, I suggest that you work from a photo of yourself, rather than looking in a mirror. You'll be able to see yourself more objectively, and you might find it easier to change some of the elements to make the composition work. You don't have to paint *everything* you see; just get your features right, and use your artistic license for the rest!

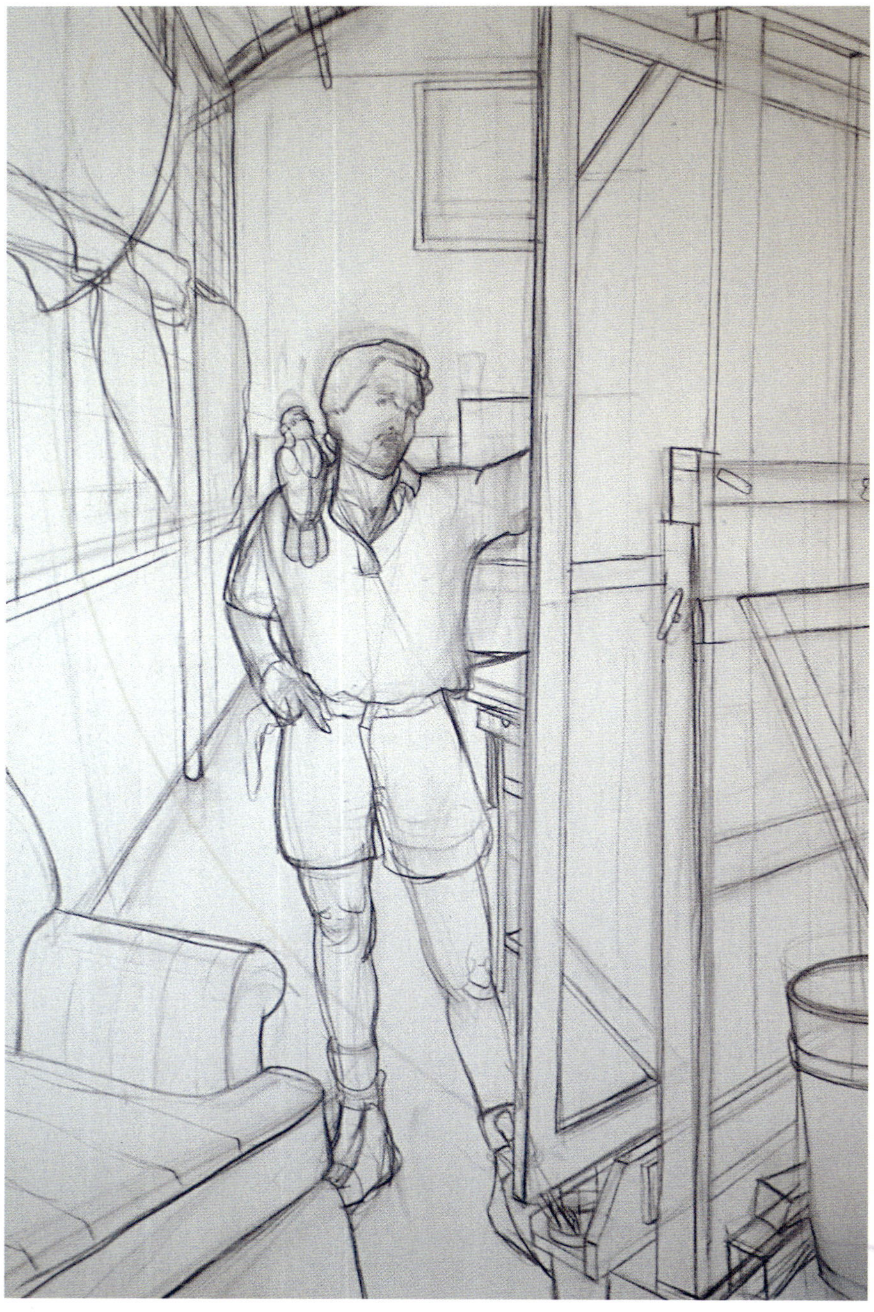

STARTING OUT First, I carefully sketched an image of myself using vine charcoal, which can be erased by rubbing it with a chamois. To get the correct perspective on the windows and ceiling, I located a vanishing point just to the right of my head and used a straightedge to find the correct angles (see the box on one-point perspective on page 25).

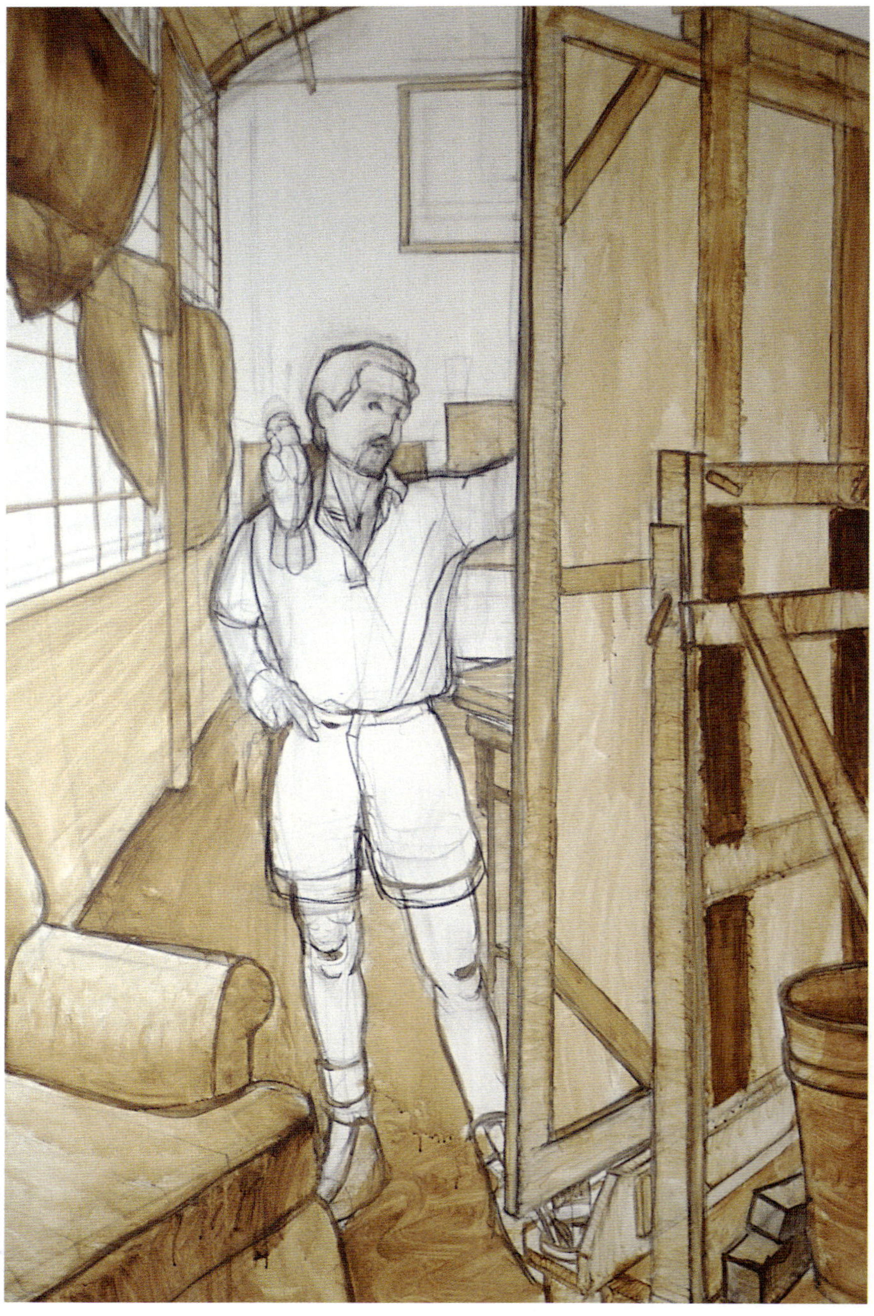

APPLYING COLOR Starting with raw umber only, I brushed in a thin underpainting, with the intention of showing it as a final, unifying color in places. Then I applied thin acrylic colors, taking care to match the values of the umber underpainting. As I painted, I continued to correct any placement problems in the drawing at the same time.

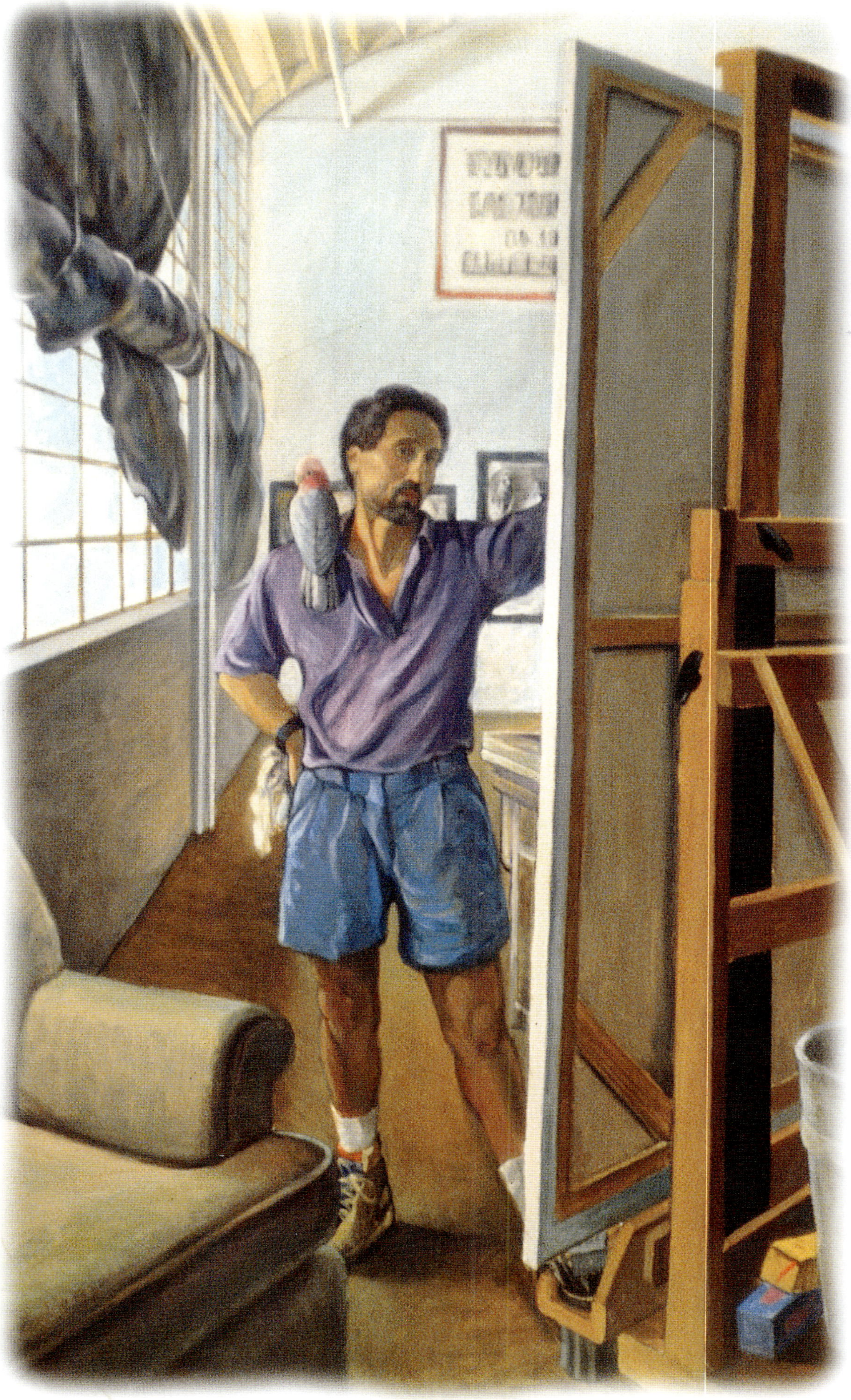

FINISHING THE PORTRAIT I used thicker strokes of paint for my clothes and completely covered the underpainting in areas where I wanted pure colors, such as the window. The underpainting shows through almost everywhere else, unifying the elements with a warm undertone.

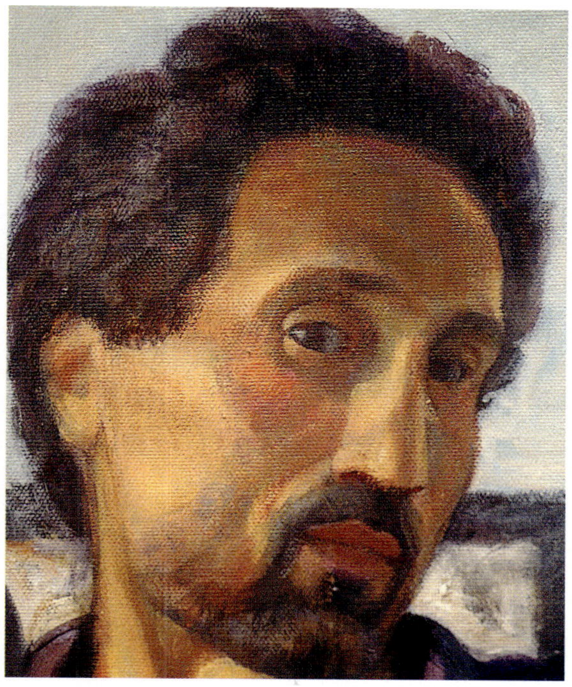

PAINTING FLESH TONES Skin tones take on slightly different hues, depending on whether they lie in light or in shadow. For the light skin tones in my self-portrait, I used a mixture of alizarin crimson and yellow ochre, with a little sap green and white. For the areas in shadow, I used the same mix of colors but in a warmer blend, incorporating more yellow ochre and green and little or no white (below).

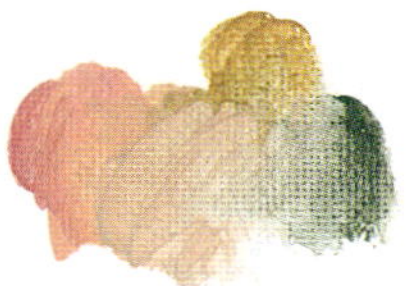

Skin tones in light

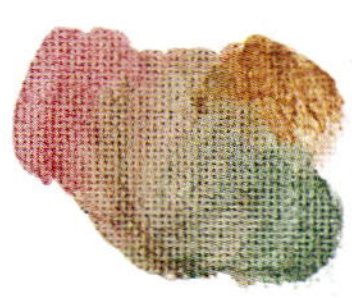

Skin tones in shadow

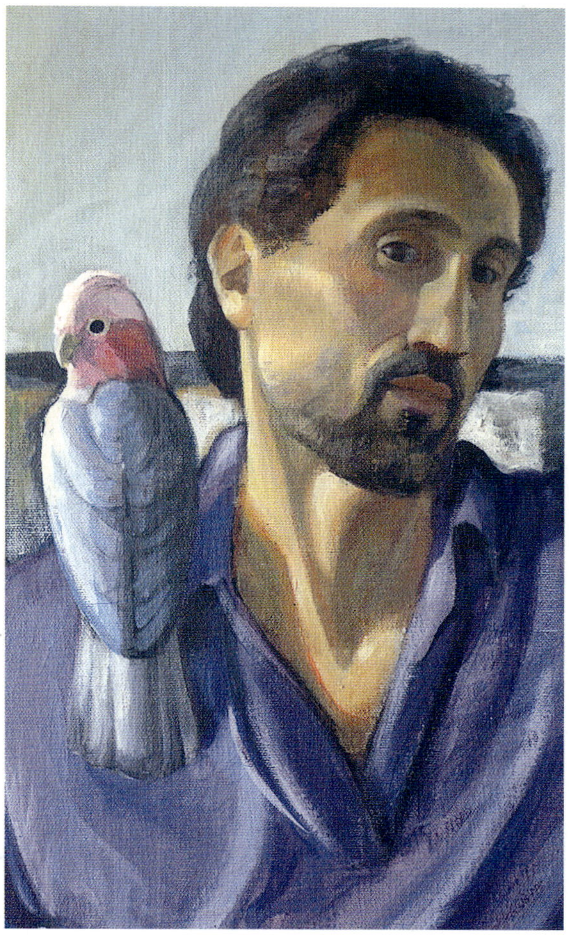

PAINTING FABRIC The lavender folds were painted with cool lights (blue-gray) and warm shadows (purple). None of the strokes were blended, so you can clearly see the light, middle, and dark value areas. I also made the cast shadow (upper right) follow the form of the folds to show roundness.

Creating Shirt Folds

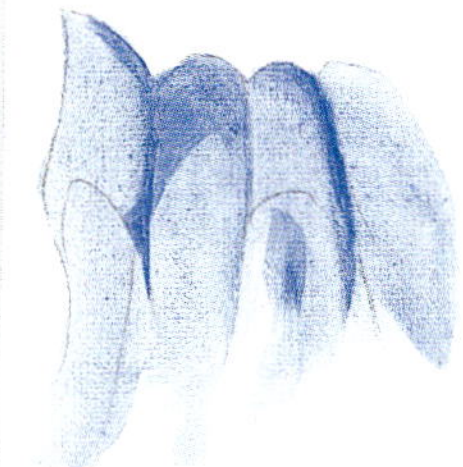

Base of diluted cobalt blue

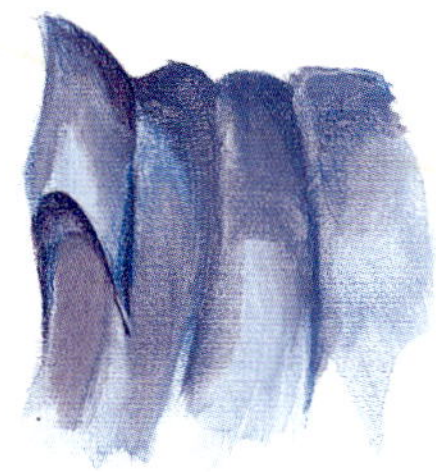

Violet added for shadows

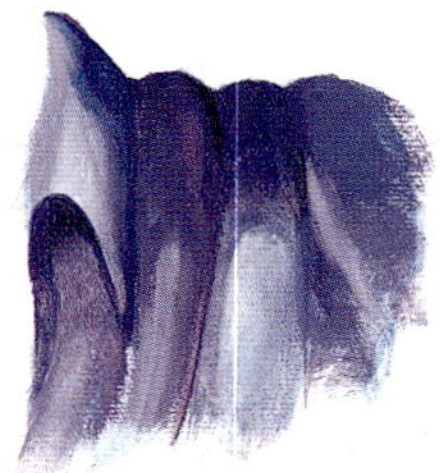

Dark violet for shadows and white for highlights

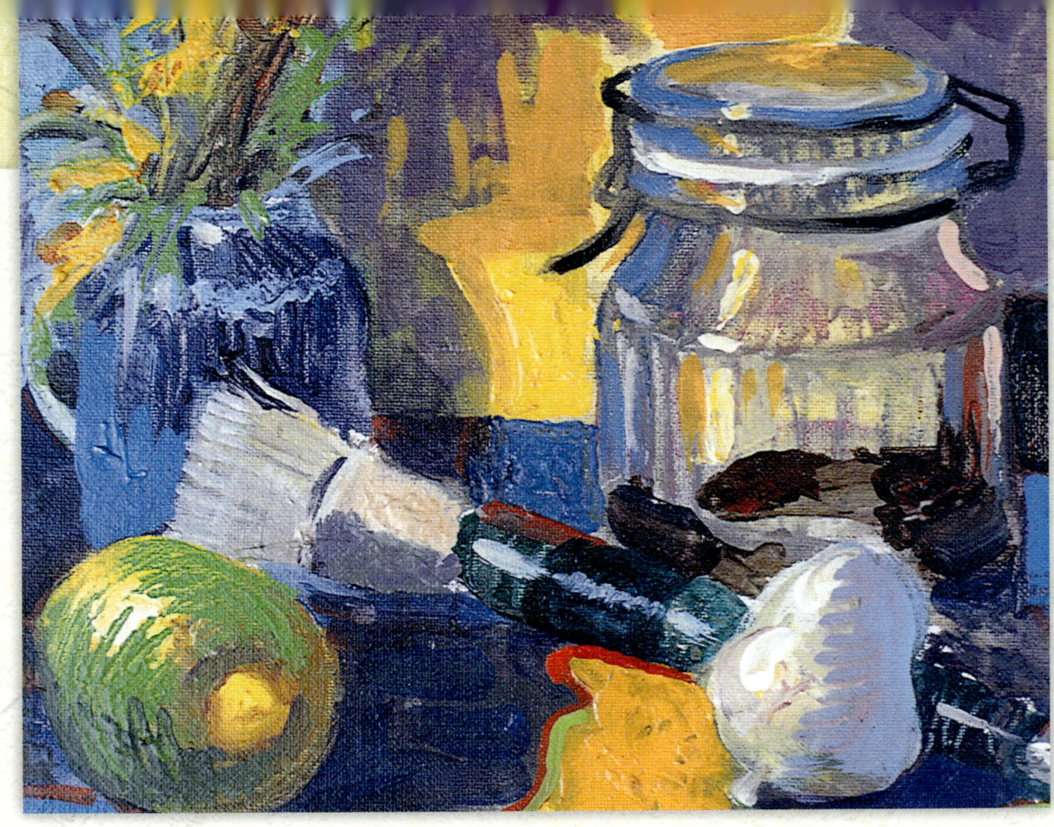

About the Artist

Ken Goldman is a popular instructor at the Athenaeum School of the Arts in La Jolla, California, where he teaches portrait, artistic anatomy, and landscape painting classes. He is also the author of four other Walter Foster books: *Pastel 1* (HT268; formerly *Starting Out in Pastel*), *Portraits* (HT240; formerly *Portraits in Pastel*), and *Landscapes* (HT242; formerly *Landscapes in Pastel*) in the How to Draw and Paint series; and *Charcoal Drawing* (AL25) in the Artist's Library series. Ken received his training in New York at the Art Students League, National Academy of Design, and New York Studio School. A recipient of numerous awards, Ken has exhibited widely in various group shows and more than 30 one-man shows in the United States, Mexico, and Europe. His artwork is featured in the permanent collections of several major museums. Ken lives in San Diego, California, with his artist-wife Stephanie Goldman.